Terrific
Makerspace Projects

PRACTICAL GUIDES FOR LIBRARIANS

⊚ About the Series

This innovative series written and edited for librarians by librarians provides authoritative, practical information and guidance on a wide spectrum of library processes and operations.

Books in the series are focused, describing practical and innovative solutions to a problem facing today's librarian and delivering step-by-step guidance for planning, creating, implementing, managing, and evaluating a wide range of services and programs.

The books are aimed at beginning and intermediate librarians needing basic instruction/guidance in a specific subject and at experienced librarians who need to gain knowledge in a new area or guidance in implementing a new program/service.

⊚ About the Series Editors

The **Practical Guides for Librarians** series was conceived and edited by M. Sandra Wood, MLS, MBA, AHIP, FMLA, Librarian Emerita, Penn State University Libraries from 2014–2017.

M. Sandra Wood was a librarian at the George T. Harrell Library, the Milton S. Hershey Medical Center, College of Medicine, Pennsylvania State University, Hershey, PA, for over thirty-five years, specializing in reference, educational, and database services. Ms. Wood received an MLS from Indiana University and an MBA from the University of Maryland. She is a fellow of the Medical Library Association and served as a member of MLA's Board of Directors from 1991 to 1995.

Ellyssa Kroski assumed editorial responsibilities for the series beginning in 2017. She is the director of Information Technology at the New York Law Institute as well as an award-winning editor and author of 36 books including *Law Librarianship in the Digital Age* for which she won the AALL's 2014 Joseph L. Andrews Legal Literature Award. Her ten-book technology series, *The Tech Set* won the ALA's Best Book in Library Literature Award in 2011. Ms. Kroski is a librarian, an adjunct faculty member at Drexel and San Jose State University, and an international conference speaker. She has just been named the winner of the 2017 Library Hi Tech Award from the ALA/LITA for her long-term contributions in the area of Library and Information Science technology and its application.

Recent books in the series include:

Terrific Makerspace Projects

A Practical Guide for Librarians

Juan Denzer
Sharona Ginsberg

PRACTICAL GUIDES FOR LIBRARIANS, NO. 67

ROWMAN & LITTLEFIELD
Lanham • Boulder • New York • London

Published by Rowman & Littlefield
An imprint of The Rowman & Littlefield Publishing Group, Inc.
4501 Forbes Boulevard, Suite 200, Lanham, Maryland 20706
www.rowman.com

6 Tinworth Street, London SE11 5AL, United Kingdom

British Library Cataloguing in Publication Information Available

Library of Congress Cataloging-in-Publication Data

Names: Denzer, Juan, 1972– author. | Ginsberg, Sharona, 1986– author.
Title: Terrific makerspace projects : a practical guide for librarians / Juan Denzer, Sharona Ginsberg.
Description: Lanham : Rowman & Littlefield Publishing Group, [2020] | Series: Practical guides for librarians; no. 67 | Includes bibliographical references and index. | Summary: "Step-by-step instructions to guide you through exciting projects for makers of all skill levels. As a bonus, find useful info on how to customize and use these projects for outreach and promotion of your makerspace, your library, or your institution"—Provided by publisher.
Identifiers: LCCN 2019057233 (print) | LCCN 2019057234 (ebook) | ISBN 9781538131824 (paperback) | ISBN 9781538131831 (epub)
Subjects: LCSH: Makerspaces in libraries. | Libraries—Activity programs. | Maker movement.
Classification: LCC Z716.37 .D46 2020 (print) | LCC Z716.37 (ebook) | DDC 025.5—dc23
LC record available at https://lccn.loc.gov/2019057233
LC ebook record available at https://lccn.loc.gov/2019057234

♾️™ The paper used in this publication meets the minimum requirements of American National Standard for Information Sciences—Permanence of Paper for Printed Library Materials, ANSI/NISO Z39.48-1992.

Contents

Preface

A significant part of the ethos behind the maker movement is sharing—skills, projects, best practices, and more. Our intention with this book is exactly that: to share details of projects we have created so they are reproducible and customizable. We hope these projects will be useful to others in the way we have often taken inspiration from others in our work with our makerspace.

At the time of writing, both of us worked at SUNY (State University of New York) at Oswego's Penfield Library, where Sharona led the makerspace and Juan frequently collaborated with her, offered ideas, and served as a backup. We created all the projects in this book together, and have had success introducing or showcasing them as part of various library events and celebrations.

Who Is This Book For?

Primarily, this book is for anyone who is interested in the projects, whether you are a librarian or not, whether you run a makerspace or not, and whether your makerspace is in a library or not. Each project chapter includes notes on possible variations, as well as a number of suggestions on how the project might be implemented or incorporated into different contexts and settings. Projects range in difficulty and in level of technology proficiency required, and anything can be modified to alter both the difficulty and technology level.

We started out writing this because we had already explored a number of books and resources on starting a makerspace and wanted more creative ideas for using an existing makerspace. Therefore, we hope this book will especially be useful to people who work in or with makerspaces that have already been established and are looking for something beyond the basics.

Due to the special nature of these projects (see "What Are These Projects?" below), this book can also be a resource for anyone interested in unique approaches to promoting libraries or other services.

⊚ What Are These Projects?

As stated, the projects in this book are made to be highly customizable and used in whatever way you'd like. Something that makes them special, however, is that they were designed as projects created by us (librarians/makerspace facilitators) rather than projects in which we guide others (makerspace users). We then showcased them during library events with the goal of promoting the makerspace, as well as other library services, while using them to build connections both within and external to the library. Exploring the "Incorporating the Project" section of each project chapter will provide you with more details on how we did this, as well as suggestions for other possible ways you might implement the projects. If our approach doesn't suit you, there are many different options, including working with makerspace users to create the projects instead.

Following our project chapters are a few bonus projects from other institutions to further develop a picture of how maker projects at varying difficulty levels created by makerspace staff can be a successful promotional tool.

⊚ How to Use This Book

This book does not need to be read start to finish, but can be explored at your own pace and in whatever order you choose. Most projects are self-contained and all necessary details are provided in its chapter. One exception is the Library Services Scavenger Hunt: some of the items following this were used in context as elements of this larger project. However, it's entirely possible to extract these projects from the scavenger hunt and create them for a different purpose. They will stand alone well, though you may want to read the initial chapter about the Library Services Scavenger Hunt to get a full picture of the element you would like to make.

Aside from the project chapters, we offer suggestions for how to guide your own growth as a maker, as well as tips and tricks that may come in handy for makerspace staff or volunteers, drawn in large part from our own experience.

⊚ Bonus Resources

Some of these projects involve writing code. To make it easier to reproduce and modify these projects, we have made our code available through GitHub. Find our GitHub repositories here: https://github.com/practical-code-for-librarians.

The 3-D prints used in some projects were taken from the website Thingiverse. We have created a Thingiverse collection grouping together these 3-D models, which you can access here to print them yourself: https://www.thingiverse.com/sg_librarian/collections/practical-guides-for-librarians-book.

Every project in this book has been created and tested in a real library setting, and this book is packed with details, photos, and resources to allow readers to use these ideas to their fullest potential. Please explore and experiment, and we hope you, too, will follow the maker ethos and share what you create!

Acknowledgments

We would like to thank the contributors who generously took time to provide information for the bonus projects section: Beth Campolieto Marhanka (Georgetown University), Don Undeen (Georgetown University), Dennis Thoryk (Onondaga Community College), Colin Nickels (North Carolina State University), Ty Van de Zande (North Carolina State University), Justin Haynes (North Carolina State University), and Adam Rogers (North Carolina State University). Thank you, as well, to our editor, Ellyssa Kroski.

We also offer many thanks to the current and former employees of Penfield Library who have helped us implement many of these projects. We are especially grateful to Bryan Schuff, who worked with us to develop the projects that involved materials from our Special Collections, and to Emily Mitchell, whose help has been invaluable for both the makerspace and for us as people.

Sharona would like to thank her family for their support, her partner Charlette for generally being an amazing person, and Kristin Fontichiaro for helping her discover her passion for makerspaces. Thank you to Chris Hebblethwaite for being an encouraging and patient mentor, and thank you to Juan for being a great friend and collaborator.

Juan would like to thank his colleague and friend Sharona. Without her, this book would never have been possible nor such a pleasure to write. She has helped him be a better maker in so many ways and be the creative person who brings joy to others. Juan would also like to thank his colleague, mentor, and friend Emily Mitchell. She kept him grounded in his regular work while encouraging him to achieve these projects. Emily was always positive of even his most far-reaching ideas and he will always be grateful.

Photo Booth/ Selfie Station V.1

⊚ Project Description

PHOTO BOOTHS HAVE BEEN AROUND FOR DECADES. The first coin-operated booth appeared in 1925 in New York City. The photo enclosure took photos of a person sitting on a stool. Prints strips were developed and ready in minutes. Their popularity grew over the years which included many in Hollywood and the art world, like Andy Warhol.

Libraries have been using photo booth setups for years. They use open-style photo booths that look more like a studio setting for a photographer. Libraries are quite creative with their "booths." Some choose to create elaborate layouts that appear to transport you back in time. Others might create picture frame walls. Whatever type of photo station they choose, libraries know how fun they can be for their patrons. They also know how well they can be used to promote their library. Promoting the library with images of users is a great way to have your library be known and seen.

In the 1980s and 1990s, the American Library Association (ALA) used celebrities to promote libraries with the READ campaign. Celebrities like Bette Midler, David Bowie, and Denzel Washington took portraits of themselves reading books. Although portraits of them reading were taken by professional photographers, they still had an inviting feel to them. They are similar to the candid selfies that appear on dozens of social media sites. Libraries have incorporate these selfie-portraits in their own READ campaigns.

⊚ Overview

This project is designed to incorporate the elements of the photo booth, selfies, and promotional campaigns such as the ALA READ campaign. It will allow libraries to make a photo booth/selfie station that is mobile and reusable. The overall projects will contain the same basic elements of photo booth that include a life-size photo frame, camera, and props.

The basic photo frame is designed so that your library can customize it for various events. The camera you will make is a throwback to old-time shutterless cameras from the 1850s with a modern twist. Instead of relying on actual photo prints, the camera will upload the images so that they can be used in your social media accounts. This is achieved with any Apple iPad or Android tablet that is connected to the internet via Wi-Fi. Others effects include making a trigger button and simulated powder-flash. Props can be made from various materials with equipment that you should already have in your makerspace.

This project is designed for all levels of skill. Construction of the frame and camera will require basic carpentry skills that anyone can do. There are no programing skills needed to upload the images.

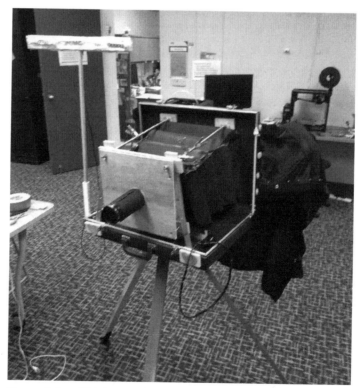

Figure 1.1. Old-time picture camera. *Figure by Juan Denzer.*

⊚ Materials List

Photo Booth Frame

- (4) 2 × 6 × 8 building wood
- (4) 2 × 4 × 6 building wood
- (4) 2 ½" zinc-plated flat corner brace
- (6) 2" L-shape zinc-plated corner brace right angle bracket
- 1 box – 3" wood deck screws
- (4) 2" service caster wheel swivel plate with locking brake
- Interior latex or spray paint (your color choice)
- Logo printed nylon fabric (optional)
- Fabric (optional)
- (2) Screen door pull handle (optional)

Camera

- Old leather/vinyl briefcase or small suitcase
- (4) 1/5 × 18" threaded rod
- (16) Nut and washer for threaded rod
- (2) Wing nuts and bolts
- (4) ¼ × 1 ½ × 12" wood strips
- (4) ¼ × 12" wooden dowel rods
- (1) 12" × 12" plywood
- (2) 1 ½ × 12" plated steel slotted metal flat bar
- Black curtain or fabric
- Non-slip thin foam padding
- Metal Victorian style costume buttons
- Black poster board
- Black large card stock paper
- Clear document protector
- (2) 2 × 2 × 8 building wood
- Apple iPad or Android tablet
- iOS-compatible selfie button wired or Bluetooth

Props

- (10–20) ¼ × 12" wooden dowel rods
- Card stock paper—80lbs or greater
- Various markers

LED Photo Booth Sign

- Battery powered mini LED String Lights (also called fairy lights)
- (2) ¼ × 12" wooden dowel rods
- White poster board
- Acrylic paint (white, yellow, brown, black)

⊚ Necessary Equipment

- Electric power drill
- All-purpose drill bit set
- Hack saw
- Wood saw
- Wood square
- Tape measure
- Sharp box cutter
- Scissors
- Sandpaper, medium grade
- Several ratcheting bar clamp/Spreader
- Screwdrivers (flat and Phillips)
- Glue gun
- Duct tape
- Miter box (optional)
- Chop saw (optional)
- Hole saw drill bit (optional)
- Electric impact drill (optional)
- Electric or manual staple gun (optional)

⊚ Step-by-Step

Photo Booth Frame

1. Before beginning the construction of the frame, measure the height of your doors and the elevator in your library. Since the frame will be adult full-size, it is important to make sure it will be mobile in your library. The frame will be six feet in height, four feet in width, and about three feet in depth. Including the base, the frame will reach a height of 6'8" to 6'10".

2. Measure out the frame with 2 × 6 × 8 pieces of wood. Measure and mark two 6' pieces of wood for the two side pieces and two 4' pieces of wood for top and bottom pieces of the frame. Take one of the 6' pieces and hold it vertically about 8" from the floor in a doorway. Make sure it will clear the doorway. If there is not enough room, cut off 5" for clearance on both side pieces.

3. Once the four pieces have been measured and checked for clearance, it is time to make the cuts. If you have access to a chop saw, use it to make clean true cuts. You can also use a miter box with a hand saw. If you are going to make cuts freehand, make a straight line as a guide for the cut. You should also use ratcheting bar clamps to secure the wood to a table or bench. When cutting the wood, begin slow and cut at a 45-degree angle to the wood. Make sure the wood is lying flat on the widest part. Do not use excessive force or speed. Let the saw do the work.

4. After all the pieces are cut, sand the edges so they are free from splinters. Lay the pieces flat on the floor and make sure they fit properly. The 4' top and bottom pieces will be placed on the inside of the two 6' pieces, so that they are flush with the 6' pieces and the frame does not exceed a 6' height.

5. Construction of the frame will consist of pre-drilling and squaring off the frame. It is important to make sure the frame is as square as possible to avoid looking

uneven. Each corner will be attached with two deck screws. Start by measuring a center point two inches from the outer ends of the 6' pieces along the 6" width. Then mark another point two inches from first point. When you are done, you should have a total of eight points marked, four markings for each 6' piece of wood. Take one of the 4' pieces of wood and make sure the markings line up with the wood. The goal is to have a mark that you will drill into and hit both the six- and four-foot pieces of wood.

6. Next, the wood pieces need to be pre-drilled. This is done to avoid splitting the wood. It will also make it easier to screw so that the screw does not overheat and snap off. Line up one of corners and clamp the two pieces down. Take the wood square and make sure the corner is true. Do this by placing the square in the inside corner. Make adjustments as needed. Once the corner is true, it is time to pre-drill. Make sure to select a drill bit that is long enough to go through and touch both pieces. It should also be smaller in size so the hole is not larger that the screw. It is important that the screw is still gripping the wood, so the pilot hole must be smaller. When drilling make sure that the drill is level and straight as possible. Most electric drills will have a built-in level. Do not apply excessive pressure as this may cause the drill bit to snap. After you have pre-drilled a corner mark the backside of each piece with "Corner #1," this will help when piecing the frame together. Then move on the next corner and mark them "Corner #n."

7. After all the corners are pre-drilled it is time to drill them in place. Line up each corner and screw them in place with deck screws. Then flip the frame over and add the 2 ½" zinc-plated flat corner brace brackets to each corner. Remember to make pilot holes for the brackets to avoid splitting the wood.

8. Now the base needs to be constructed. The base is an H-shaped structure with four caster wheels and wooden supports for the back. Measure out and cut the following pieces of wood:
   A. 1 – 2 × 4 × 6' cut in half—two three-foot pieces
   B. 1 – 2 × 6 × 8' cut into one four-foot piece
   C. 1 – 2 × 4 × 6' cut into one four-foot piece
   D. 2 – 2 × 4 × 6' cut into two sets of one four-foot piece and one sixteen-inch piece

9. Take the B piece and lay it flat. Place the frame on top vertically flushed long ways. Mark a line on B along the entire length. This will be the guide line for piece C. Place C on top of B so it is flush and the four inches of the 2 × 4 is vertical. The goal is to create a T-frame that the larger frame will sit on.

10. Clamp B and C together and pre-drill holes for deck screws. Each hole will be drilled from the bottom of B. Space the holes six inches apart, starting with the first hole six inches from one edge.

11. Next add legs to the base to make an H-shaped structure. Mark 18 inches on each leg, part A. Place one leg on opposite sides of part B perpendicular to each other. The backside of B should be flush with the mark on A. Pre-drill holes from the bottom of B into A. Use two deck screws for each leg.

12. Place the large frame on a flat table and clamp it down. Secure the base to the bottom of the large frame. Pre-drill holes from the bottom of the base (B) and into the frame. Space the holes about six inches apart as previously described. Pre-drill holes from the backside of the base (C) into the frame. Be careful not to fully drill a hole all the way through. Part C should be secured to the frame without having the screw punch though.

13. L-shaped wooden brackets are needed to keep the frame stable. It will also help when moving the frame. Create two L-shaped brackets with parts D. Use the same method used for the large frame. Make sure the corner is four inches wide and not two.

14. Attach the bracket to the frame and base. Position them on opposite sides so that they are an upside-down L. Use 2" L-shape zinc-plated corner brace right-angle bracket to secure the bracket to the frame and base. Each wooden end should be secured with two right-angle brackets.

15. Once the frame is attached to the base, it is time to paint the structure. Choose a favorite library color and either use latex or spray paint.

16. Finally, add 2" service casters to the base. Make sure to pre-drill pilot holes.

Figure 1.2. Moblie backdrop frame. *Figure by Juan Denzer.*

Camera

1. Begin by cutting a square on the top of the briefcase. This should be about the size of the clear document protector. This window will be used so the user of the camera can see the picture subjects in the frame.
2. Drill two holes above the cut-out window. The holes should be opposite each corner. Attach metal rods and use two nuts per rod to secure them in place. They should be sticking out long enough so they reach the front of the suitcase when opened.
3. Next, take the steel-slotted metal flat bars and mount one to each rod. This will act as support for the wooded front plate that will hold the iPad or Android tablet. Use nuts to secure them. Then secure the bottom of the bars to the inside of the briefcase.
4. Use the wooden strips and plywood pieces to make the front plate of the camera. The iPad or Android tablet will be mounted between the two pieces of plywood. Make two-square frames out of wooden strips. Mount the plywood to one of the square frames. Use a strong bonding adhesive on the wooden frame and plywood. Drill four holes in each corner of the wooden frames. Make sure the frames are lined up when drilling the holes. The holes should be large enough for the metal rods and bolts to pass through. Add non-slip foam padding to the insides of the frame. This will help protect the iPad or Android tablet as well as keep it from slipping out of the fames. Place the iPad or Android tablet on the inside of the plywood with the camera lens touching the wood. Measure where the camera lens touches the wood so that a small hole can be made to let the iPad or Android tablet take images. The frames will sandwich it and hold it in place.
5. Use heavy black cardstock to make camera bellows. The bellows will be hot glued to the inside of the briefcase so it covers the cut-out window. The other end of the bellows will be glued to wooden front plate.
6. Make a fake camera lens out of black poster board or heavy cardstock. The lens is just for aesthetics. Be creative and mount it to the wooden front plate with a glue gun.
7. Take the black fabric and drape it over the top of the suitcase above the cut-out window. Use hot glue to secure it. Add some metal buttons to give it a Victorian look. Use the wooden dowels to prop the fabric up. This gives the camera a more inviting appeal.
8. Cut three equal legs out of wood to support the camera. They will act as a tripod. Make sure they are equally balanced on the bottom of the briefcase so that it is stable. They should be permanently mounted to the bottom using a strong bonding adhesive or hardware.

Props

1. Props are fun and easy to make. They are cutouts made of card stock and wooden dowels.
2. Start by drawing out different shapes. Fun shapes include things like glasses, monocles, mustaches, beards, ties, etc.
3. Use a box cutter or scissors to cut out the shape.
4. Attach a ¼ × 12" wooden dowel to the cutout with hot glue. For added security use duct tape to ensure the dowel will not fall off.

LED Photo Booth Sign

1. Start with a marquee silhouette cutout from construction paper. Use this as a template to cutout a sign from poster board.

2. Mix acrylic paint to create a wood color mixture. This will be painted on the marquee sign. Slowly mix the colors white, brown, and yellow to get a desired color. Test your paint on a scrap piece of poster board. Paint the entire front of the sign.

3. Next create text that you can print on a printer, or paint it freehand with acrylic paint. There are lots of fun fonts that can be used for the sign.

4. Add LED lights to the sign. Measure the perimeter of the marquee and divide by the number of LEDs in the string of lights. This will give you the distance between each LED. Take a pencil and ruler evenly mark LED points around the back of the sign. Use a thin nail to poke a hole for each point. Poke all the way through. Take the pencil and make a lager hole for the LED, make sure to punch from the front of the sign.

5. Push each LED through a hole from the back of the sign. Use the glue gun to secure the LED. Attach the battery back to the back of the sign with duct tape.

6. Add ¼ × 12" wooden dowel rods wooden dowel to the sign. Attach them with duct tape.

7. Measure the center of the photo booth frame and center the sign on that mark. Mark where the dowels touch the frame. Then drill two ¼" holes where the dowel can be inserted. This will allow the sign to be attached/removed for transport.

Lessons Learned

The photo booth/selfie station proved to be a challenge for the makerspace. It began with a simple idea that went through a lot of improvements. It was also developed for a specific event within a few weeks. Although there was some initial planning and drawings of the frame and camera, much of it was done through trial and error—which is not uncommon in makerspaces.

Much of the adjustments were improvised during the event and right after. When working on a project as big as this one, it is important to keep track of issues. It is also important to keep track of what works as well. The improvements can be carried over to other projects. For instance, the frame initially used PVC piping to add supports. Although PVC was acceptable, it was not an ideal solution. Adding L-shaped wooden brackets were much more stable. The knowledge we gained from creating L-shaped wooden brackets can be used for other projects.

Variations

Photo Booth Frame

Some variations to the frame include adding screen door pull-handles. This makes it easier to grab onto when transporting. It also will keep hands from handling the painted surface. Another alternative to a painted frame is to use fabric. The fabric can be wrapped around the frame and stapled in place. This adds a nice textured artistic feel to the frame. Nylon fabric can also be added the back of the frame. Several companies do logo printing on nylon sheets. We had ours printed by Spoonflower. This is a great way to add a backdrop to the frame. It is similar to the backdrops seen at events where celebrities are photographed.

Camera

One possible variation to the camera is to add a flash bar using LEDs. They can be synched to flash when the iOS camera button is pressed. An easy way to add the flash button is by using a wired momentary button that can be mounted on top of the iOS button: when the user presses both buttons at the same time, they will work in sync. Another variation is to add a large display to the camera. Images can be cast to the display, then those taking a picture will see themselves on the display.

Props

There are so many ways to add variation to props. Hats and scarfs are a great way to add fun to the photo booth/selfie station. Thrift shops are great places to find some of the most interesting items. They include things like funky hats to funny glasses. Several cosplay items can be used.

Another great way to add fun props is to use a Silhouette Cameo or other vinyl cutter. Use it to make oversized cutouts of maker tools such as a hammer, screwdriver, or knitting needles. They can be glued to pasteboard and cut out. This will make them reusable.

LED Photo Booth Sign

Using actual wood makes a great variation. It gives the sign a real solid look and feel. It may require more advanced woodworking skills and tools such as a band or jig saw. Also be sure to use a thin soft wood, it will make it easier to work with when making holes.

Using multicolored lights creates a nice effect. This can be done easily by adding an additional string of color lights. Then alternate them when attaching them to the sign. Flickering lights are also a fun, eye-catching effect.

◎ Incorporating the Project

This project can easily be incorporated to any library event that wants to see patrons engage with the library. It is a great tool for social media. Since the station and camera are mobile, they can be transported just about anywhere.

◎ Key Points

- Photo booths are a great tool for getting people to interact with each other.
- The photo booth/selfie station is completely mobile. This allows libraries to use it at any event. Additionally, it is very customizable for all types of events.
- With the popularity of selfies, people are more comfortable taking candid photos of themselves.
- Social media has made it easier to upload and share images with each other.
- Libraries will benefit from this type of photo booth. Rather than having instant gratification of images, patrons will have to access the library social media site to obtain the pictures. This helps to draw users to the library's web presence.

AR (Augmented Reality) Scavenger Hunt

Project Description

SCAVENGER HUNTS ARE A STAPLE of library events and activities, but incorporating AR (augmented reality) technology can take things to the next level. Augmented reality is a technology that takes advantage of devices with cameras, such as smartphones, to overlay digital information on the physical world. The popular mobile game Pokemon Go is an excellent example of AR, as players can point their phone cameras at various real-world locations and reveal hidden Pokemon creatures they can then interact with through the game's interface. Including AR in a scavenger hunt event can not only engage library users, but can also be a fun way to introduce people to this relatively new technology and show them its capabilities.

Creating a fairly basic AR scavenger hunt is a much simpler task than it may seem at first. In this scavenger hunt, participants seek out images printed and placed in specific locations, then scan the images with their smartphones to reveal related text or another image. Some ideas of how to effectively use this project will be covered in the "Incorporating the Project" section; it's a very versatile framework that can be utilized for a wide variety of different goals.

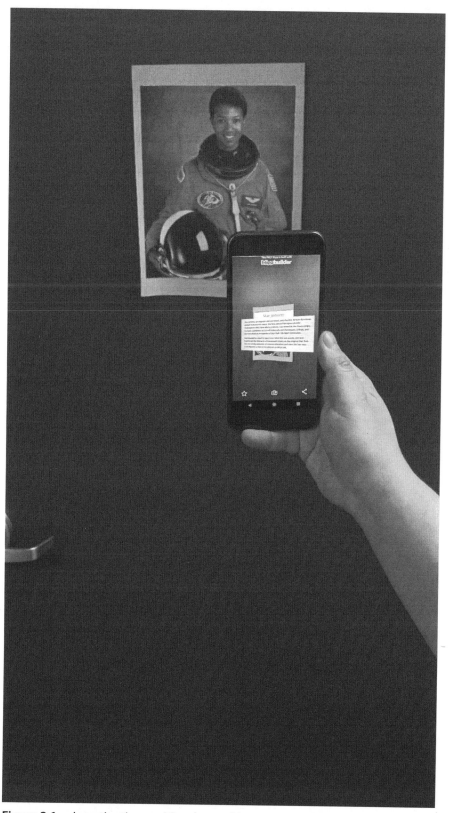

Figure 2.1. Investigating an AR-enhanced image. *Figure by Juan Denzer.*

ⓖ Overview

There are a number of free AR apps out there, and which ones exist or what features they have are likely to be in constant flux. This project can be accomplished using the app Blippar, and this chapter will outline how to use this specific tool in its current form, but it's easily adaptable to other similar applications and tools.

The project will involve choosing a theme, planning and preparing paper clues, and creating linked content through Blippar's website. A little bit of comfort with technology is ideal, but there is no programming or deep understanding of AR required, so by no means do you have to be a technology expert to carry it out. In fact, it functions fairly well as an introductory AR project.

ⓖ Materials List

- Copy paper, construction paper, and/or cardstock for printing physical clues
- Glue, tape, other craft materials

ⓖ Necessary Equipment

- Computer with internet access
- Smartphone or tablet running iOS or Android*
- Participants in the scavenger hunt will need their own smartphones or tablets (or a group may share a device)*

*Note: More information about what devices can be used to run the Blippar app can be found by viewing the app on the Apple App Store or the Google Play Store. In our testing of this project, we successfully used modern phones such as Samsung Galaxy S5, as well as an older iPod Touch.

ⓖ Step-by-Step

1. Choose a theme or purpose for your scavenger hunt and develop content. What are the clues participants will be searching for? What additional content will the clue reveal once it's found?
2. Once clues and information to reveal have been plotted out, create the physical clues. These are the images you will post in the area where you will construct your scavenger hunt. An easy approach is to print the images on regular printer paper and back them with colored cardstock using an ordinary glue stick.
3. Create a Blippar account. At https://www.blippar.com, click the "Signup" link and create a free account. You will then be able to log in and access the Blippar Hub dashboard, where projects are stored. Click "+ New Project" to start and name a new project, then click "Create a Blipp" to start on your first clue.
4. Blippbuilder is the tool you will want to choose for creating your clues or "blipps." Select and upload one of the images you have selected to be a clue (one of the same images you have already printed and prepared). This image is referred to as your marker. You can name the blipp and continue.

5. There are various elements and widgets Blippar offers as possibilities for what will be revealed when participants scan the blipp. For this first project, keep things simple and stick to the Text element and the Take a Selfie widget, which you can manipulate to display a single image. To place an element or widget, drag and drop it onto the marker you uploaded. A number of configuration options will appear on the right-hand side of the interface.

Figure 2.2. An image loaded into the Blippbuilder to serve as a marker. Elements can be added by dragging and dropping from the menu on the left. *Screenshot from BlippBuilder at blippar.com.*

6. To ensure your content will be easily viewable against the background, and since the Text widget doesn't allow for a background color, use word processing software or text editing for a quick workaround. Write your content in an ordinary document (as with Microsoft Word, Google Docs, TextEdit, Notepad, etc.), take cropped screenshots, and use those screenshots as images in the Take a Selfie widget.

To do this, drag and drop the Take a Selfie widget onto the work area, or what Blippar calls the canvas. (The Gallery widget also adds images, but we could not find a way to eliminate the navigation arrows that come with it, so we went with the Take a Selfie widget instead.) On the configuration panel on the right, click "Add a background image" and upload the screenshot of your text from the word processing document. If the image doesn't appear in your canvas, try clicking "Add a background image" again and switch over to the "Uploads" tab to find the uploaded image and select it. You can then drag to resize the image (zooming in and out from the lower right corner of the work area if needed). You can also tweak certain settings using the configuration panel, such as opacity, scale, and the positioning of the image in three dimensions. Again, keeping things simple in this first project, let the image lie flat (Z = 0 for position) and make it just a bit bigger than your marker.

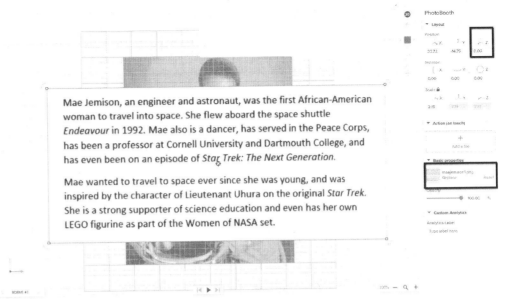

Mae Jemison, an engineer and astronaut, was the first African-American woman to travel into space. She flew aboard the space shuttle *Endeavour* in 1992. Mae also is a dancer, has served in the Peace Corps, has been a professor at Cornell University and Dartmouth College, and has even been on an episode of *Star Trek: The Next Generation.*

Mae wanted to travel to space ever since she was young, and was inspired by the character of Lieutenant Uhura on the original *Star Trek.* She is a strong supporter of science education and even has her own LEGO figurine as part of the Women of NASA set.

Figure 2.3. Upload an image as the "background" and set the Z position to 0. Move and resize the image as needed. *Screenshot from BlippBuilder at blippar.com.*

7. You may use the Take a Selfie widget (or any other widget) as many times as you'd like. In this project, each marker uses it twice: once for the title (name of the person) and once for the description (short bio).

8. From here, in the paid version of Blippar, you can choose to Publish your blipp and make it widely available. In the free or educational version, you can't publish and make the blipps live. However, what you can do is allow users to access the blipps using a test code.

   Back out of editing the blipp and return to viewing your project, with the interface displaying each blipp you have created. At the bottom of a blipp, there is a small, three-dot icon. Clicking it will display a menu, where you can select "Publish to Test." Enter a code and click the Continue button. A screen will appear that should display your test code and the marker from the blipp you were editing. Click "Publish to Test." You will need to do this for each blipp/marker and enter the same code in order to link them all. Picking a memorable, easy-to-type code is ideal, as people will need to enter the code on their devices later in order to participate.

9. To test your blipps/markers, download the Blippar app to a testing device, such as a phone or a tablet. The device will need a camera and internet connection through either WiFi or mobile data. When you open the app, you will need to allow it camera permissions, but you should not need to allow location for it to work.

   Once the app has fully started, look for the settings (a gear icon). In the settings, there is an option to enter a test code. Here, you can type in the test code you created when editing your blipps on the website. This will allow you to access the linked content you created for each marker/clue. If you were to scan a clue without entering this test code, Blippar would not recognize it and be able to display your content.

Figure 2.4. Entering a test code in the app. *Screenshot from Blippar iOS mobile app.*

10. With the app open and the test code entered, hold up your device to point at one the clues you created in step 2. If everything has been done correctly, your linked content should pop up overlaid on the feed from your camera.

When preparing directions for your scavenger hunt, be sure to explain to participants how to enter a test code on the app so they will be able to duplicate this process.

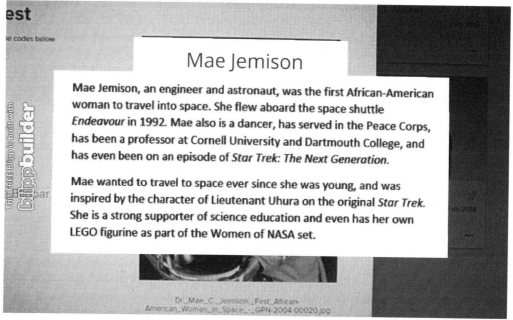

Figure 2.5. Testing the marker to see the information appear. *Screenshot from Blippar iOS mobile app.*

⟲ Lessons Learned

The most important takeaway for us in carrying out this project was that some participants may need some kind of motivation or incentive to engage with the AR. In order to accommodate people without smart devices, we posted our linked content in physical form near our clues, as well. Those who chose to could lift the paper flap and read the content rather than using the Blippar app to scan the image. Since this was a lower barrier method that involved less exploration of new technology, many of the scavenger hunt participants went for it instead. In the future, we would look for a different way of providing content to those without smart devices, and would think about how to get participants more excited about downloading a new app and trying out the AR. We do believe the technology has a lot of potential, and that it's important to help patrons learn about and develop digital competencies, so the trick may be in tweaking the design of the project to get people more excited about engaging.

⟲ Variations

The basic framework of this project is very versatile and can be adapted to all kinds of different goals and events. Though we opted for a scavenger hunt, the same technology could be used to develop interactive exhibits or displays, even allowing for visitors to point their cameras at physical objects or locations to reveal additional information or interactive content. For this project, we stuck to the very basic elements and widgets in Blippar, as well as basic types of clues/markers. More advanced versions could ask participants to scan objects or locations with their device cameras and could incorporate features like videos, animations, audio files, PDFs, or even social media content. Although we didn't test these features ourselves, Blippar should be able to handle clues/markers such as photos of objects, book covers, or locations taken from a specific angle (where participants could then be told to stand with their devices).

An important challenge to consider when creating any project with Blippar or AR in general is how to approach accessibility. Participants in your scavenger hunt, display, exhibit, or so on may be limited by not having access to an appropriate device or may face barriers due to a disability. How will you ensure that someone with visual impairments can take part or be offered an equivalent experience? You may need to develop an alternate method of completing the scavenger hunt (such as through audio clues/content) or provide the content linked to your clues in a number of different ways. Of course, be sure to keep in mind our takeaways from the Lessons Learned section to consider how to approach these alternate methods without discouraging participants from engaging with the AR technology.

⟲ Incorporating the Project

This is a project that works well to enhance library events, help participants explore, or teach participants the history of an area or service—just to name a few ways it could be used.

- Enhancing library events: This is the approach we used for incorporating the project. Our library annually partners with our local chapter of Zonta International, an organization focused on empowering women, for an event called Maker Madness. This event features tables of volunteer "makers" who demonstrate creative skills or lead interactive STEAM (Science Technology Engineering Art Math) activities. The event is also intended as a celebration of International Women's Day. To play on this theme and to contribute to the educational value of the event, we developed our scavenger hunt to focus on significant women in STEAM. Examples included Sally Ride, Ada Lovelace, Mae Jemison, and Chien-Shiung Wu, among others. Our printed clues were photos of these women, while the linked Blippar content was short biographical blurbs of text on each woman and her contributions. Participants were able to go around the library in the vicinity of the event and discover each posted clue on walls, pillars, and so forth, then read the related content to learn about each woman. By incorporating the project into an existing library event, we helped emphasize the theme of the event, as well as including an additional interactive, fun, and educational element.

• Help participants explore: Rather than keeping the scavenger hunt confined to a specific area, the project could instead be used to help participants explore. As an example, academic libraries often have new students complete orientation activities at the start of the school year, which may include a library tour or other method of learning about the library building. By searching for clues, then scanning them to learn more about a specific location, students could build their knowledge of library services and the building, or even of the campus as a whole. Much as the Pokemon Go mobile game rewards players for investigating many different real-world areas, this type of scavenger hunt makes learning about the library more of an adventure.

• Teach participants history: This type of AR scavenger hunt could be used to showcase material from the library Special Collections/Archives, or any local materials the library holds, while teaching participants local history. The scavenger hunt area doesn't even have to stay confined to the library building itself, but could expand into nearby streets, businesses, and so on. To set up the project, prepare Blippar by using current photos of specific locations—for example, the library reference desk. Participants will need to point their device cameras at the location from the same angle, but once they do, they can reveal hidden content such as an old photo of the reference desk from many years ago, an audio recording discussing the history of reference services offered, a video of a reference desk interaction, or really whatever content you can come up with. The same method could be used for participants to learn more about the history of their local community, streets, buildings, and so on.

These are just three ideas of how an AR scavenger hunt may be incorporated in a way that engages and educates participants. The project is an excellent opportunity to promote and teach about services the library offers, and to help make library events fun and rewarding.

◎ Key Points

- Augmented reality is a relatively new technology that can be used effectively in a project that is both enjoyable and informative.
- Despite drawing on high tech methods, actually carrying out this project doesn't require a high level of technology savvy. It's also a very low-cost project without complex tools and supplies.
- Participants in the scavenger hunt can scan a clue with their smart devices to reveal hidden linked content, such as text, images, video, and more.
- This project has a wide variety of possible applications, especially if you choose to move beyond the very basic features of Blippar outlined in this chapter.

◎ Resources

- Blippar (blippar.com)
- Blippar mobile app (available on iOS and Android)

CHAPTER 3

Personalized Template Bookmarks

<table>
<tr><td colspan="2" align="center">**IN THIS CHAPTER**</td></tr>
<tr><td>▷</td><td>Project Description</td></tr>
<tr><td>▷</td><td>Overview</td></tr>
<tr><td>▷</td><td>Materials List</td></tr>
<tr><td>▷</td><td>Necessary Equipment</td></tr>
<tr><td>▷</td><td>Step-by-Step</td></tr>
<tr><td>▷</td><td>Lessons Learned</td></tr>
<tr><td>▷</td><td>Variations</td></tr>
<tr><td>▷</td><td>Incorporating the Project</td></tr>
</table>

◉ Project Description

IT'S NOT UNCOMMON FOR LIBRARIES to give away free bookmarks to patrons as a method of advertising the library, its services, or other relevant local/on-campus services. Providing patrons with personalized bookmarks can be an even more memorable method of promotion, and patrons are more likely to hang onto these special bookmarks and think back positively to their experience at the library. This project can be repurposed multiple times with different templates and themes, making it highly versatile, and is a relatively low-cost and low-tech option for a maker project and a way to engage in some valuable library outreach.

This project is best carried out as part of an event, a special day, or a workshop at the library, though this chapter will explore some other possibilities in the "Variations" section. Some computer savvy and comfort with image editing is required, though you need not be an expert, and there are simple tools to help you along. At the very least, however, you will want to do a little practice and become comfortable with the tools you're using before setting out to offer individualized bookmarks to patrons.

Figure 3.1. Sample of a bookmark created for a Banned Books Week event. *Figure by Sharona Ginsberg.*

The general idea of this project is pre-creating a template or a number of templates with space left open to insert photos. During an event or workshop, participants can have their photos taken, and you can quickly insert these into the existing templates, then print them custom bookmarks to take home. Though the idea is fairly simple, the personalized touch makes the bookmarks into attractive library swag, and may even help increase your promotional outreach, as participants may want to give them as gifts or share them with friends and family.

⊚ Materials List

- Cardstock
- Laminating pouches (optional)

⊚ Necessary Equipment

- Computer with internet access
- Color printer capable of printing on cardstock
- Smartphone with a camera
  - The smartphone should have a method for uploading photos to the cloud, such as Google Photos, iCloud, etc.
- Laminator (optional)

⊚ Step-by-Step

1. Choose a location where you will take photos of participants. If desired, you may create a backdrop for people to stand in front of, or you might simply find an area that will work well as the background of the photos. We recommend choosing a backdrop or location that isn't too busy or flashy, so it will not distract from the rest of the bookmark's design. If you decide to create a backdrop, you might consider including your library's name and/or the name of the event in some way.

2. Use graphics software to design at least one bookmark template. You are aiming for a design that is focused around the borders of the bookmark—especially the top and bottom—so you will be able to place the participants' photos in the center.

   For this step, you may use any software or app you're comfortable with, keeping in mind that you will continue to rely on this tool for manipulating the participants' photos onto the templates. Here are a few of our recommendations:
   - Adobe Photoshop or Adobe Illustrator (advanced and paid software, appropriate only if you're already familiar with them)
   - Pixlr Editor (a free, web-based tool similar to but simpler than Photoshop)
   - Canva (a free, web-based option appropriate for beginners)
   - SumoPaint (a free, web-based tool similar to Pixlr)

   New tools and software are released all the time, and doing a search for "Photoshop alternatives" or "free image editing software" will yield many results and lists, so feel free to explore and experiment to find an option that works well for you. Most importantly, you'll want to use an image editor that allows for layers, so you can position the photographs correctly in your template.

Figure 3.2. A bookmark template with a transparent background created using Adobe *Photoshop. Screenshot of Adobe Photoshop.*

3. If desired, you may create more than one template so participants have options to choose from. Some elements you may consider including are the name of your library and/or institution, the name of the event (if applicable), a year, a message or slogan, a logo, or a hashtag.

4. If you'd like to give participants more than one copy of their bookmark, simply create another document in your image editor and set up a few outlines the size of the bookmarks. Later, you can copy and paste the bookmark image into each of these outlines to quickly produce a sheet of bookmarks.

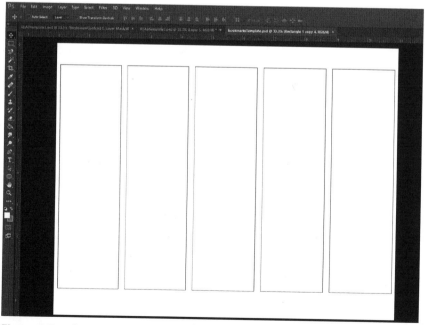

Figure 3.3. Create a document with space for multiple copies of a bookmark if you want to provide patrons with more than one. *Screenshot of Adobe Photoshop.*

5. Setup for the event will include two stations. Station one: backdrop or area where participants will pose for photos. One helper is needed to hold the smartphone and take photos. The phone should be configured to automatically back up photos to the cloud through Google Photos, iCloud, or a similar method. (Note: this will take up a lot of data! It will be preferable to stage this somewhere where the phone can access a WiFi network instead of using cellular data.) If you'd like, you may offer props or signs for the participants to hold in the photos.

   Station two: bookmark design and printing. Set up a computer (laptop if portability is required) and a printer it's connected to, either through a cable or a network. Load the printer with cardstock. On the computer, open your template(s) in your graphics program, as well as a browser window with Google Photos, iCloud, or whatever tool you're using to backup the photos. If you have multiple templates, print out samples of each so participants can view them and choose.

6. The process should run as follows: Participants pose for a photo, the camera person takes a photo with the smartphone, and the photo uploads itself to the cloud. On the computer, download the photo from the cloud-based storage, open it in your graphics editor, and copy-paste it into the bookmark template. Resize and crop as necessary to make an attractive bookmark. If you prepared a sheet for multiple bookmarks, copy-paste the entire bookmark image onto that document however many times is necessary, and arrange these images to fit. Print the document onto cardstock and you will have a sheet of bookmarks to offer the participant, which they can cut out themselves.

7. If you want the bookmarks to be sturdier, you might offer the option for participants to laminate them (after cutting them into individual bookmarks). However, this isn't strictly necessary, and does add to the cost and complexity, so it's an optional step.

Lessons Learned

Charge your phone in advance! Alternately, or in addition, have a backup smartphone or portable charger. It may seem obvious, but it's easy to forget and leave yourself without any options when the phone you're relying on for photos dies.

Though this project is relatively simple and doesn't use some of the flashier maker technology, we found it was popular and engaging for patrons—so much so that we had to create a waiting list for people as we worked through creating the bookmarks. You might consider setting up a similar list. If you're comfortable with the software you choose, it shouldn't take longer than a handful of minutes to create each bookmark, but taking photos is still quicker. Have patrons write down their information in the order they arrive. We also asked them to write down which template they wanted, and a basic description of what they were wearing, so we could easily link up the photos to the patrons without knowing their names. It may also be beneficial to have a helper to manage the list and explain it to people as they arrive.

Something we discovered about Google Photos (which may also hold true for iCloud and other photo backup methods) was the need to occasionally trigger uploads. Although Google Photos was configured to automatically upload any photos taken by the phone, it sometimes waits to do this, especially if you are taking many photos in a short period of time. Simply opening the app generally triggers the upload without an issue, but it had to be done periodically to ensure quick transfer of the photos. Be sure to test this in advance and make the camera person aware if they will need to do this.

This is a project that relies heavily on internet access; have a backup plan for technical difficulties. With any luck, you won't need it, but it's best to be prepared. Have a cable available to transfer photos to the computer manually, if need be. Have a method of connecting the computer to the printer through a cable, as well, in case the network goes down. Doing these things manually may slow down the project and make it more complex, but it's important to know what you will do in the event that you run into these difficulties in the middle of the process. Uploading photos will take a large amount of data, so it's recommended to carry this out in an area that the phone can access a WiFi connection.

Something we didn't anticipate in initially planning this project was that participants might want to take photos with friends. The templates were mostly designed to fit a single person, and although we were able to work with group photos, it was trickier. Consider designing wider bookmarks than normal to accommodate group photos, and participants will surely appreciate it.

Variations

This project was originally designed to be planned in advance, then carried out during an event or special occasion, but there are other possibilities. If you want to offer these bookmarks as an ongoing promotional item, you might have the templates on hand and have patrons inquire if they want one. You could also have the templates available in the makerspace, and have makers create their own personalized bookmarks, rather than setting this up as a staff- or librarian-led project.

On a similar note, you could use this project to teach patrons image editing and manipulation by leading them through the process and allowing them to do the hands-on work of creating the templates, as well as the bookmarks. You could also engage patrons in the creation of a photo backdrop, if you choose to include one.

We first envisioned this project as part of a Banned Books Week event (read more about this in the "Incorporating the Project" section), but there are many possibilities and variations, as you could design your bookmark templates any way you'd like and to focus on anything. Photos might feature patrons in costumes for Halloween, a Comic Con–style event, or an event that incorporates cosplay. Participants might be holding their favorite book, or a sign listing a reason they love the library. Photos could be of people's pets, or their favorite maker project. If you're at an academic library, the bookmarks might be based around staff or faculty and their research interests. Get creative, and consider what might work well for your library and your community of users.

Incorporating the Project

This project works especially well as part of an event, for educating patrons, and to help patrons celebrate or enjoy what the library has to offer.

- As part of an event: We first created this project to be carried out as part of an annual Banned Books Week event at our library. We were inspired by ALA's READ posters and bookmarks, but wanted to add a more personalized touch. Our Banned

Books Week event is a collaboration between the library and the college's Creative Writing department, so it was also a good opportunity to impress and do some outreach to the campus faculty and staff. As the event normally consists of multiple stations and activities, it was easy to add our bookmarks as another activity, and for participants to wander among the other offerings while waiting a few minutes for their bookmarks to be done. The project added a great interactive element to the event, and was definitely a draw for students, staff, and faculty alike.

Figure 3.4. Setting up this project during an event is fairly simple and effective. *Figure by Juan Denzer.*

- Educating patrons: This project could be undertaken simply for fun or for outreach, but it's also designed to easily incorporate some educational elements. During our Banned Books week event, we printed out images of the book covers of various popular or well-known banned books. Participants were then encouraged to grab the cover of their favorite banned book and hold it up for the photo. This was a very successful approach, as we experienced many students asking questions about Banned Books week and why books were banned, or expressing surprise that certain books had been challenged. By carefully choosing a theme and props, a backdrop, or designs that emphasize the same ideas, you can use this project to spark curiosity and create opportunities to educate participants or raise questions about a topic important to your library.
- Celebrate and enjoy the library: Whether you integrate this project into an event, have it available in the makerspace, run it as a workshop, or any other variation, it's an effective way to remind patrons of what the library has to offer. You could focus your bookmarks on specific library services or resources, or use them as

an opportunity for patrons to share why they care about the library. With the permission of participants, you might even share some examples of the created bookmarks on library social media to expand their reach and help advertise the library makerspace, the event or focus of the bookmark, and the library's fun and creative side.

◉ Key Points

- This is a relatively low-cost and low-tech maker project that works well for incorporating into library events, but has other uses, as well.
- Comfort with image editing is required, but there are good beginner options that can be learned fairly quickly.
- Templates are prepared in advance, then participants can have photos taken and quickly developed into personalized bookmarks.
- The project is versatile and can be used for outreach, education, celebrating library services, teaching image editing skills, and more.

◉ Resources

- Pixlr Editor: https://pixlr.com/editor/
- Canva: https://www.canva.com/
- SumoPaint: https://www.sumopaint.com/
- Google Photos: https://photos.google.com/
- iCloud: https://www.icloud.com/

Special Moments Recording Station

Project Description

VIDEO AND AUDIO CREATION AND EDITING are common activities supported by makerspaces, and many libraries offer equipment or other resources to help patrons make their own multimedia. In this project, patrons supply the content but the recording station itself can be created internally by library staff to help engage and encourage participation from visitors. The recording station doesn't require a lot in the way of equipment and know-how, and taking advantage of the Mac operating system's built-in automation tool goes a long way toward making the recording experience as frictionless as possible. This project is versatile, as the moments or stories patrons are asked to share can vary widely, and can be adjusted to fit the theme of events, special occasions, or even just focus on the library's overall values.

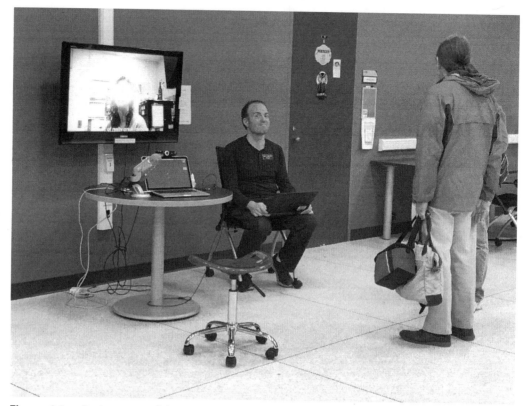

Figure 4.1. Basic set-up of the Special Moments Recording Station. *Figure by Lillianna Kiel.*

Overview

While this project may be a bit more on the high-tech side than some others in this book, once it's put into place, operating the recording station requires only a very basic level of technology knowledge or comfort. The setup requires a computer (desktop or laptop) with an extra monitor or screen attached, as well as a place for patrons to sit or stand while they make their video recordings. The general process of operating the recording station works as follows: patrons approach the station while others' clips are playing on the extra monitor, pause the clip playback, click a large record button, and make their own recording. Once finished and saved into the proper folder, their recordings join the existing playback playlist, which can be restarted. The recording station gives users the feeling of adding their voices or their stories to a growing collection.

Materials List

- Paper or cardstock for signage

Necessary Equipment

- Mac OS X computer
- Chair or stool

- Large monitor or TV screen
- Cable to attach computer to monitor/screen
- USB microphone*
- Webcam*

* optional depending on other equipment; see more notes in Step-by-Step

Step-by-Step

1. Get a computer running Mac OS X and make sure it has both QuickTime and iTunes installed. Both should come standard with the operating system, but are available for free from Apple's website in case the computer does not have them.
2. Open the application Automator, which should come with your operating system and be located in the Applications folder. This automation program will be used to create a one-click button to start a recording.
3. When presented with a choice for type of document, select "Application" and click the "Choose" button.
4. On the left side of the program window, there will be a list of Actions you can select for your automated process. Select the "Movies" category and find the option, "New Video Capture." Drag and drop this action into the large empty space on the right side of the window to build the workflow of your automated process.
5. Save your workflow (File > Save) and place it somewhere easily accessible, such as the Desktop of the computer. You may want to name your process something that will be clear to patrons, such as, "New Recording,"

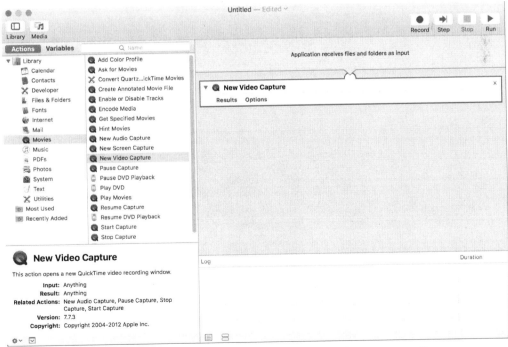

Figure 4.2. Setting up actions in the Automator. *Screenshot of Automator software.*

6. A step that isn't strictly necessary but will add to the appeal and clarity of your automated process is to change the icon to make it look like a button. To do this, first find a button image you would like to use. (Note: Try sites with public domain images like Pixabay or look for public domain clip art.)

Once you have found and downloaded an image, open it in an image viewer of your choice. Select the entire image (the keyboard combination Command + A usually works, or look for the option in the program's menu). Copy the image (Command + C or Edit > Copy).

Go back to the file you created with Automator and open the Info window (Control + Click and select "Get Info"). Just to the left of the name of your file will be a small icon you can click to select. Once it's selected, use paste (Command + V or Edit > Paste) to replace the icon with your copied button image.

7. If desired, you may also choose to make your icon larger and more prominent. If you've placed it on the computer Desktop, go up to the Finder (Desktop) menu and choose View > Show View Options. Once this window opens, you will be able to adjust icon size. Note that this will increase the size for all icons on the desktop, so you may want to clear anything not needed before proceeding.

8. Test your button. When you double click the file you created with Automator, the computer should open a new QuickTime movie recording window. Starting the recording will simply require users to click the round red record button on QuickTime's controls.

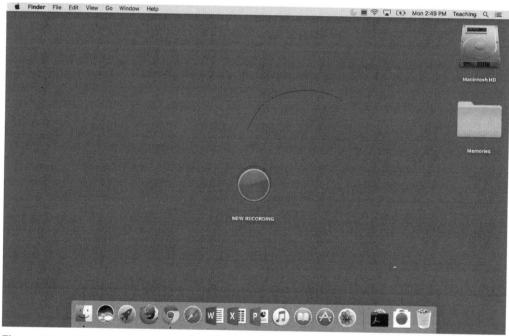

Figure 4.3. Set up a simple interface with large and minimal icons. *Screenshot of computer desktop.*

9. Create a folder where recordings will be saved. This may be placed anywhere you would like.

10. Open iTunes and create a new playlist (File > New > Playlist). You can name it anything but remember what you called it.

Next, go back to Automator and this time create a Folder Action rather than Application. Find the action "Import Files into iTunes" under the Music category, and drag/drop it into the workflow area. You can then adjust the settings to have files saved to the "existing playlist" you just created.

11. Above this in the workflow area, you will see a drop-down menu where you can choose what folder this automated process will act on. Browse for and select the folder you created to save recordings. Save your process (File > Save).

    At this point, whenever a user saves a recording in QuickTime to the folder you created, the recording will automatically be added to your iTunes playlist and will be included in the looping videos being displayed as part of the recording station. This prevents you from having to manually add each video to the queue once the recording is finished.

12. Give the whole process a quick run-through to test it. It should work as follows:
    a. Patron double-clicks your "button" for a new recording. A new Quicktime movie recording window is opened.
    b. Patron clicks the red record button in Quicktime and records themselves speaking. When finished, they click the stop button.
    c. Patron saves recording (File > Save) to the designated folder. (Note: Once a file is saved to this folder from Quicktime, this should be the default save option for subsequent files unless manually changed.)
    d. Recording is automatically added to iTunes playlist.

13. If everything is working as intended, you may set up the physical space of the recording station. Whether you use a USB microphone or external webcam is up to you; some computers may have mics and cameras already installed, while some may not. Even if your computer already has these devices built in, it may be worth it to use the external devices for better sound and video quality, especially in noisier areas, but it's not required if you don't have access to them.

14. Connect the computer to the large monitor/screen with the appropriate cable and adjust settings so different things are displayed on each screen, rather than the screens being mirrored. You can access these settings under the Mac's System Preferences > Displays. Drag the iTunes window to the large monitor and hit play to begin the video playlist. To have the playlist loop when finished, you can toggle the repeat button on controls on top of the iTunes window. If someone would like to make a recording, simply pause the video playback until they are finished.

Lessons Learned

You will likely want to have at least one person on hand to help patrons operate the recording station. Though the setup is intended to make things as easy as possible, having a helper to explain the process and pause the playback of recorded videos is ideal.

Another consideration is making some videos in advance to pre-populate the playback queue. It's not necessary to have a lot, but it's helpful to have something playing at first to interest people before the first patron recordings have been made.

Accessibility can be tricky for this project, as there is no existing tool we know of that will automatically and accurately caption videos without any human intervention. Any pre-recorded videos used to start off the station should certainly have captions added before being used. If you plan to save videos and make them available in any way, captions should be added; there are certainly tools that will attempt to automatically apply captions, such as YouTube, but they will need to be reviewed and adjusted by a human before being shared. For further accessibility, make sure your recording station setup is flexible enough that people with different heights and bodies can reach the equipment. Having an external microphone and webcam is helpful for this, as you can adjust them more easily than a computer's built-in mic or camera.

If you choose to incorporate this project into an event with other offerings, think carefully about how you organize your space and what else you have available. If every other activity is quick or doesn't involve participants staying in one location for an extended period, it might be more difficult to encourage people to linger long enough to make a recording. Additionally, if the recording station is surrounded by things that are flashier and more immediately attractive, it might be difficult to catch people's attention for long enough to have them make a recording, as well. Plan the incorporation of the project thoughtfully.

⊚ Variations

This project relies on having a computer running Mac OS X since it takes advantage of the operating system's built-in Automator tool, as well as QuickTime's simple video recording option. It's possible the project could also be carried out with a computer running a different operating system, such as Windows or Linux, if comparable software is available. While we have not explored this, we encourage makers to experiment and find additional tools to make the project work for them.

Rather than using this station to capture video recordings, you might vary it and collect audio recordings instead. QuickTime can also be used for audio, so the setup would be largely the same, simply switching out the result of the Automator workflow you create to begin a new audio recording rather than video recording. If you choose to go this route, make sure to consider accessibility by providing text transcripts alongside shared recordings.

The physical setup of this project is fairly simplistic and, aside from the screen displaying the recorded videos, meant to be unobtrusive. If desired, you might get more creative with the appearance of the recording station, adding backdrops, props, or special design elements to enhance the theme you choose or to grab attention more effectively.

⊚ Incorporating the Project

- As part of an event or physical exhibit: This recording station was originally created to serve as one activity among many during our library's 50th Anniversary Celebration event. To fit our theme, we solicited special moments and memories about the library from visitors. In adding this project to an event or exhibit, you may ask participants to share thoughts on any theme, from library services to favorite books to current events, and more. The station provides a fun, interesting way for patrons to engage with the library and have their voices heard. If you choose to make this recording station part of your event or exhibit, consider what will happen with the videos afterward, and if you will share them somewhere for others to experience (see next bullet for suggestions). If you plan to do this, explain it as part of the process to patrons and obtain permission to share their recordings after the conclusion of the event.

- Digital repository or digital exhibit content: Many libraries, especially academic libraries, have digital institutional repositories where they store and present library materials. Some libraries also have platforms they use to create digital exhibits that can be accessed from outside the physical building. While the recording station itself can be a fun project, your focus might be less on the experience of making recordings and more on sharing these recordings through one of these methods. If you pursue this, don't forget to consider accessibility and captions as mentioned earlier in Lessons Learned.
- If your library uses social media for promotional purposes and to interact with patrons, you might incorporate this project into a social media campaign. The recording station might be set up over a more extended period (rather than a shorter period as for an event), and patrons encouraged to use it to create a video that will be shared through social media. People who aren't able to visit could contribute by creating their own videos and tagging the library. For example, during Banned Books week, patrons might record a short reading from their favorite banned book, or participants could speak about why the library is important to them during National Library Week.

⊚ Key Points

- This project takes a little technology comfort to set up, but is fairly easy and frictionless to run once prepared.
- Participants can use the recording station to add their voice and thoughts to an ongoing stream of video clips.
- This recording station project fits well with events, exhibits, digital collections/repositories, social media campaigns, and more.

⊚ Resources

- iTunes documentation: How to Play, Repeat, and Shuffle: https://support.apple.com/en-us/HT207230
- Automator User Guide: https://support.apple.com/guide/automator/welcome/mac
- How to Change Mac OS X Icons: https://www.wikihow.com/Change-Mac-OS-X-Icons

Magic Radio

Project Description

MANY LIBRARIES HAVE A SPECIAL COLLECTIONS or archives department. There is so much rich history that comes in many formats. They not only include books and manuscripts; they also include a lot of audio recordings. Libraries spend so much time and money digitizing these recordings so they can be made available for patrons. The digital recordings are often made available online for scholars to hear. It is one of the easiest and most common ways to provide this content. This project provides a more tactile and engaging way to bring audio recordings to patrons. Rather than having patrons just mouse click their way through an online-interactive experience, the project gives them a way to experience recordings that were simple yet so powerful long ago. By using an old radio that creates the effect of coming alive when a point is touched, the radio will give the ghostly effect of tuning into a radio station to play an audio recording.

Although this project can be used as stand-alone, it is best suited for an exhibit type of display or a library event. It can be used as an alternative listening device for a larger display. The project might not draw as much attention when used alone. It will vary from many of the other projects in this book; the radio that is used is not specific to one particular model. This allows for you to tailor the model you choose that fits the exhibit or event. For instance, the project might call for a 1950s-style radio. This project will also be challenging because not every radio is shaped the same, and the tuning needle and knobs might be different. This challenge will also help in sharpening up your maker skills.

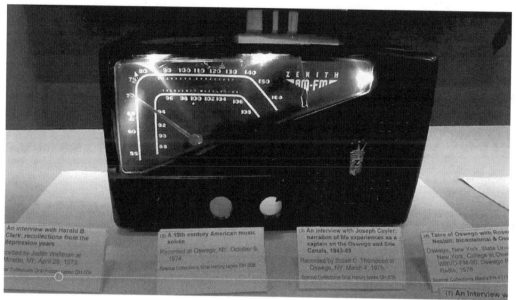

Figure 5.1. Magic Radio. *Figure by Juan Denzer.*

The general idea of this project is to create a radio that "auto-tunes" to a random radio station and play an audio recording. The radio does not actually tune into a radio station; it merely gives the effect of it. It does this by using servos to rotate the dials on the radio. LED lights are added to give it a glowing effect while white-radio noise plays before the actual recoding is played. Patrons will be able to press touch points to make the radio come "alive."

⊚ Materials List

- Any old radio that uses round dials and a needle-style tuner
- One Bare Conductive Touch Board (www.bareconductive.com)
- One Arduino Uno R3 board
- Mini breadboard
- Two SG90 micro servo motors
- Several male-to-male jumper wires of various lengths and color
- Several super bright white 5mm LEDs or pre-wired LED strings

- One small battery powered speaker with 3.5mm input audio jack
- Two USB cables to power each Arduino board with chargers
- One 3.5mm audio cable
- One micro SD card capable of storing all the audio recordings for the project
- Standard size poster board
- 2–3 – 1" × 2" × 6' wooden boards
- Spool of single-stand wire, 16–18 gauge
- Several size screws non-coated
- Acrylic paints (optional)
- Resistors for LED wiring (optional)
- Several 5mm LED holder solderless https://www.thingiverse.com/thing:170562 (optional)
- Touch Board Case https://www.thingiverse.com/thing:1454954 (optional)
- Arduino Uno R3 Case https://www.thingiverse.com/thing:101985 (optional)

Necessary Equipment

- Solder Kit
- Glue gun
- Strong bonding adhesive
- Duct tape
- Saw for cutting wooden board
- Wire stripper
- Screwdrivers, both Philips and flat-head
- Utility cutting knife

Step-by-Step

1. The most difficult part of this project is choosing the right radio that fits the budget and the theme where it will be used. You need to take special consideration when choosing a radio. It should be big enough inside to fit servos, LEDs, wiring, mini speaker, and the circuit boards. Also, choose a radio that has a clear enough front for the tuner. The goal is to be an able to add LEDs that will give the radio a glowing effect. Make sure the radio has a large enough straight tuning needle. Do not choose one that is a bar-type tuner. This type will not work well at all. Also, be sure the tuner range is short. The servos are programmed to have limited movement for a short time. Finally, consider using a radio that has old vacuum-type tubes. When LEDs are added to the tubes, it makes for a great ghostly effect.
2. Begin this step by removing all the inner components of the radio. There should be enough clearance to fit all the electronic components. Keep the parts that will be used in the project. This will include all the radio knobs and tuning face place and needle. If you are using a radio that includes vacuum tubes, try to preserve as many tubes as possible, if it requires removal of the needed parts, remember how it can be put back in later.

Figure 5.2. Magic Radio in 50's theme. *Figure by Juan Denzer.*

3. The two SG90 micro servos will need to be mounted to the audio and tuner knob on the radio. Mounting each servo will take some ingenuity. It is not difficult, but it will take some trial and error to get it right. Most older radios will have some sort of pulley system for the tuner knob. When the knob is rotated, it will turn another wheel that moves the tuner needle. If the radio has this type of system, attach the servo to the back on the knob inside the radio. If the tuner knob is more complex, it might be best to connect the servo directly to the tuner needle from behind. Remember to center and align the servos directly behind the knob of turner needle. If they are not centered, the servo will not rotate freely and it will get stuck.

4. Next, find a place inside the radio where the speaker will fit and clearly be heard. Look for a location where there are holes or slits. Since the speaker is battery powered, it might sound muffled if placed in a location that is blocking the sound. Make sure that you can switch the speaker on and off. Plug the 3.5mm audio jack into the speaker input and the other end into the touch board.

5. Take either a pre-wired strand of LEDs or create your own LED strand with LEDs, wires, and resistors. Place the LEDs inside where they can been seen when the radio is active. A good place for the LEDs is near the tuner strip of the radio.

6. Carefully select the audio recordings that you will want to play on the radio. Remember to keep them relatively short, no more than 30 seconds. The touch board is only capable of 12 touch points. The recordings should be in mp3 format. Format the SD card so that it is completely empty. An SD card that has others files might interfere with playback. Label each audio file with the following format:

TRACK000.mp3, TRACK001.mp3, TRACK002.mp3, and so on. TRACK000.mp3 will correspond to the touch point number 1. TRACK011.mp3 will correspond to the touch point number 12. Once the mp3 files are created, copy all of them into the root directory of the SD card.

7. Find a good location for the two Arduino boards and the mini breadboard. The mini breadboard should go in between the two circuit boards. Make sure the boards are easily accessible and secured inside the radio.

8. Once all of the components inside the radio are connected and working properly, you can mount the radio. The radio will need a platform for the touch points and wiring. Depending on the size and shape of the radio, lay out a piece of poster board that is large enough to fit the radio and room for all touch points. The points need to be well spaced apart with about a few inches from each other. Since the system uses capacitive touch, the points need some distance from one another to avoid having inference when a point is touched. Once you have the poster board laid out, cut it into either a rectangle or square shape. Then create a bottom frame for the poster board with the wooden boards. Use a strong bonding adhesive to connect the frame and mount the poster board to it.

9. Next, mark the touch points on the poster board. Start by measuring single strand wire from each point in the touch board to the corresponding point on the poster board. The wires will run underneath the poster board and be secured by duct tape. When running the wires, avoid crossing them as much as possible. Crossed wires may lead to interference and cause the points to not correspond correctly. The wires can be attached to the touch board by using a non-coated screw and wrapping the stripped end of the wire. The other stripped end of the wire will poke all the way through the poster and lay on top. It can be covered by acrylic paint or a sticker that says something like "Press here." Mount the radio onto the poster board and use hot glue to secure the radio.

10. Once all the wiring is done, it is time to upload the code to the Arduino. The code is available from a special GitHub repository specifically written for this book. Download the Arduino source code and upload it to the board. Test to make sure the system is working correctly.

11. Finally, connect the USB cables that power the two Arduino boards. Find or make an external slot for the cables. Zip tie the cables together and plug them in to the chargers. Power up the radio, test, and enjoy.

⑥ Lessons Learned

One of the most challenging steps for this project was making the tuner needle rotate in a way that makes it appear as if it was tuning into a station. A lot of trial and error was done to get the timing right. Unlike other projects where the main component is either a standard piece of equipment or something that can easily be swapped out for something else, the radio we were working with not only fit the theme, but also we had already begun working on it. So there was no room to change it. We also were on a tight schedule and didn't have the time to go looking for another radio. Other challenges included securing the servos to the tuning knobs from inside. We realized that servos need to be aligned well. Over time, if the servo is not centered on the knob, it will create stress on the servo. This leads to no movement or the servo breaking off.

Although this project may seem complicated, it is relatively simple in design and implementation. Much of what looks complex is actually just a few servos that cause the radio knobs to move. All of the code runs on two Arduino boards. We learned that it is much easier to have an all-in-one circuit board such as the Bare Conductive Touch Board to handle the touch point and audio playback. We also learned that it made more sense to separate the servos and have them run on one Arduino board. The challenge we discovered was getting the two boards to sync when a patron touched a point.

Something we discovered about using touch points and how we marked them: We used our university color and made a round circle with acrylic paint on poster board. As the event went on, the paint stated to crack. We also realized that even though we labeled each dot with a title of the audio recording, patrons generally didn't know what to do with it. They were not sure what to do with the radio. Even children who generally are curious in nature and enjoy touching things did seem to understand. It would have been better if the dots we labeled "Press here." We wanted to avoid having a sign with instructions as that would have taken away from the nostalgia.

This is a project that relies a lot on ingenuity that every maker has in them. It was a great way for us to sharpen our maker skills. We went through a lot of iterations for making the servos move the tuning needle. They require some precision when aligning them up to the knobs. Much of the materials we used ended up being replaced by something else. What made the challenge fun was coming up with a solution that worked.

Something we didn't anticipate initially was how much care it takes to store the radio. Since we were on a tight schedule for the 50th anniversary, we were not thinking of long term. We also we not thinking of how well the radio would hold up, even for the event. We were more concerned with making sure the radio was able to play the recordings. Looking at the project after the event we realized it would have been better to think long term.

Variations

There are so many variations for this project because it does not rely on one specific main component. What makes it unique is the radio you choose. It can be from any era or fit any theme. You can choose one that is nostalgic or chose one that is futuristic.

This project can be used in so many ways because it touches on several senses. Patrons are not just presented with a two-dimensional web page that plays audio files. They can see and touch a three-dimensional object that stimulates the senses while playing an audio recording. The radio by itself is not going to draw people. It is just a prop that needs a theme. A backdrop or set where patrons will be drawn in by curiosity or nostalgia is best suited.

Incorporating the Project

This project works especially well as part of an exhibit or event, for educating patrons, and to help patrons celebrate or enjoy what the library has to offer.

- As part of an event: This project was added to one of many stations as part of our library's 50th anniversary. We converted a small group study space into a late 1950s to early 1960s den area. The radio was the main focus of the den. It was placed on a table with a large screen behind it. The screen was playing a virtual fireplace.

The study space walls were decorated with curtains. There was an old phonograph, lamp, vacuum, suitcase, and chairs. This helped create an inviting place that patrons were curious to see and gave them a sense of nostalgia.

Figure 5.3. Bottom of radio before removal of components. *Figure by Juan Denzer.*

- Educating patrons: The audio files were specially chosen by our library's special collections librarian. They carefully chose audio recordings that were from fifty years ago and represented the university at the time. This included recordings from student and faculty. The goal was to have patrons learn a little about the university history. Some patrons looking over the title and names of those recordings might have remembered hearing about it. Other younger patrons might have been excited to hear about was going on fifty years ago.
- Celebrate and enjoy the library: Libraries are a great place for people to learn something new. It is a great place to experience new things as well. This project can be used in many different ways to promote the library. It can be used as part of an exhibit to showcase part of the collection. Use it at event to promote the specific theme of the event. Place it in the library children's section to spark interest for children.

Key Points

- Depending on where you acquire the radio, this can either be a low-cost project or high end.
- Some steps will require a little more ingenuity that cannot be shown in the steps written here.

- This does require some basic soldering skills.
- This does require some basic electrical skills.
- The audio files are easily interchangeable that require no change in Arduino code.
- The project is versatile and can be used for many different types of exhibits or events to promote the library.

⊚ Resources

- Bare Conductive Electronics: www.bareconductive.com
- GitHub Arduino-Magic-Radio repository: https://github.com/practical-code-for -librarians/Arduino-Magic-Radio

Photo Booth V.2

Project Description

THIS PROJECT IS A VARIATION OF CHAPTER 1'S PHOTO BOOTH. Instead of using an iPad to take the pictures, this version uses a Kinect device with a laptop that capture images and places a backdrop in the image. This is all done in real-time and does not require any post-image manipulation. Images taken by the camera are ready to share just as they are in chapter 1.

Overview

This project is designed to incorporate the elements of the photo booth, selfies, and promotions such as the ALA READ campaign. It will allow libraries to make a photo booth that is mobile and reusable. The Kinect has a camera that can filter objects in the foreground and remove the background. This project allows for a digital background to be inserted in real-time.

The platform is designed so that the camera, laptop, and Kinect are well supported. The camera is lightweight and easy to set up. It has an access panel that allows access to the laptop. The Kinect is mounted on the front which allows for easy adjustments.

This project is designed for all levels of skill. Construction of the platform will require basic carpentry skills that anyone can do. There are no programming skills needed to capture the images. No post-image editing software is required to create fun images with a digital backdrop.

This version of the camera is not only updated in the design, but also the theme of the camera has been updated. It has a more contemporary look that younger patrons automatically identify with and thus they are drawn to the camera.

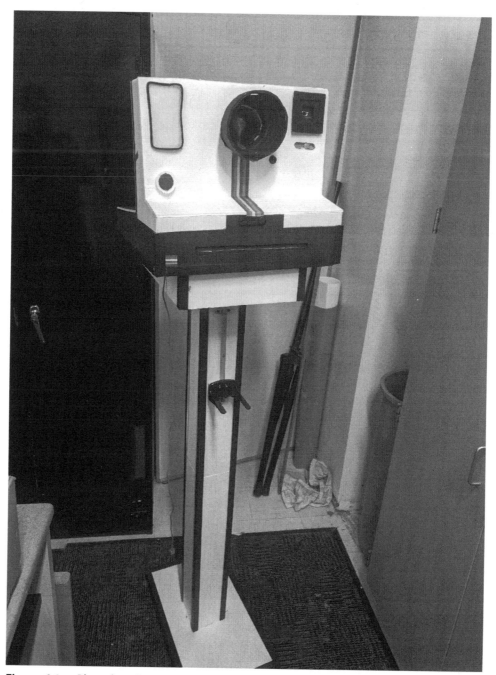

Figure 6.1. Photo booth camera version 2. *Figure by Juan Denzer.*

Materials List

- Several sheets of black and white poster board
- Laptop running Windows 10
- Xbox 360 Kinect or Kinect for Windows
- (3) 2 × 4 × 6 building wood
- (2) 24 × 24" plywood
- (4) 2" service caster wheel swivel plate with locking brake
- Box of interior deck screws about 2" in length
- Velcro strips with adhesive backs
- Large zip ties
- Small flat neodymium magnets (optional)
- Spray paint or latex paint (optional)

Necessary Equipment

- Electric power drill
- All-purpose drill bit set
- Hack saw
- Wood saw
- Wood square
- Tape measure
- Sharp box cutter
- Scissors
- Sandpaper medium grade
- Several ratcheting bar clamps/Spreaders
- Screwdrivers (flat-head and Philips)
- Glue gun
- Duct tape
- Miter box (optional)
- Chop saw (optional)
- Hole saw drill bit (optional)
- Electric impact drill (optional)

Step-by-Step

1. Start by building the platform for the camera. Measure the 2 × 4 building wood so each beam is about 4' in length or about neck height on the average adult. The platform should be tall enough so that children are not able to poke the camera but are able to see it. Stack the beams together long length wise. When looking from the top or bottom the beams should form an "I" shape. Use the deck screws to secure the column together.
2. Take the two pieces of plywood to create the base and top for the platform. Center the column and secure one piece of plywood to the bottom of the column. Use deck screws to secure the plywood. Drill holes into the plywood for cable to pass through. Make the holes large enough for the USB connector of the Kinect and

the power cable for the laptop. Make holes on the top and base. Place them a few inches from the column.

3. Once the platform is complete, add four caster wheels to the bottom. Paint it if desired. For a nice aesthetic look poster board is an inexpensive solution that is easy to apply. It will give the platform a museum type look. Cut and shape the poster board and use hot glue to mount it. Add some plastic trim to hide the seams if desired.

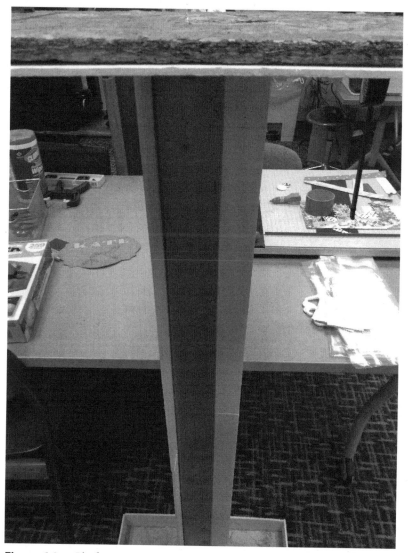

Figure 6.2. Platform with poster board cover. *Figure by Juan Denzer.*

4. This step will involve taking a 3-D image of a camera and printing out a template in 2-D. The camera in this project is iconic and there are several websites on the internet where a 3-D image of it can be found. Once a 3-D image is found, it will need to be printed in 2-D from all sides. Once all side are printed, measurements will need to be taken and doubled or tripled depending on how big the prints are made. Take all the outer measurements to create panels that will be glued together. Keep in mind that the camera will be a 3-D object. It might be easier to use cardstock and cut out each panel. Then create a small mockup. Take notes of sections that need special attention. The only side of the camera that should not have a panel is the bottom. This is so the camera fits over the laptop which will be laying on top of the platform. Another approach is to make a template for all

the panels by enlarging the image sections at a time. This is done with a copier to print on larger paper. Start by taking a printed panel and dividing it into four equal sections. Cut up the sections into individual pieces. Use the zoom feature on the copier to enlarge each individual section to a size that will work. Do that for each individual section and then stitch them together with tape. Once the template is stitched, cut it out to make a template. Then it can be drawn on poster board and cut out. Do this for all the panels of the camera and glue them together. Do not glue the back of the camera. That panel is for easy access to the laptop. That panel can be held in place with small magnets. When all the panels are glued, add a nice camera lens made of plastic cups or poster board. Decorate the camera with paint and other accessories to make it look convincing to patrons. Add some Velcro strips to the bottom of the camera and to the top where the camera will rest. This will keep it secure and prevent it from being knocked over.

5. Next, use the extra pieces of wood to create a small shelf for the Kinect. The Kinect should be between 2–3 feet from the floor. A simple shelf can be made by cutting a long enough piece of 2 × 4 wood that will support the Kinect. Cut a triangular-shaped wedge to support the shelf. Attach the wedge to the wooden column and use a strong adhesive to bond the shelf and wedge. Use zip ties to secure the Kinect to the shelf.

6. Finally, download and install the Kinect for Windows Software Development Kit (SDK) version 1.8 and the Kinect for Windows Developer Toolkit version 1.8. The code for this project is available from a special GitHub repository specifically written for this book. It has further instructions of how to install and customize the application for your needs.

ⓖ Lessons Learned

This version of the photo booth station was still a challenge for the makerspace even with the lessons learned from version 1. The biggest challenge was making the mock camera. It required finding a 3-D image of the camera and printing out all sides in 2-D. Since the camera was larger than what can be printed on paper, a lot of basic math was involved to determine the percentages.

All the crafting to design the camera and platform was much easier for this project. That was due to all the lessons learned from working on version 1. We also were not on a tight schedule. This allowed us to build a system that is easier to store, transport, and set up. This version can be set up in matter of minutes, unlike the original version that takes some time to set up. This version is easier to run and power. The back cover is easily removable in case the software or computer needs to be restarted.

One big lesson we learned while running the event was how the Kinect reacted to multiple subjects. Our makerspace student, Alexander (Alex) Lawrence, discovered that it was difficult to capture more than one person at time. It was even more difficult when there were three or more people. Most of the images would cut people off, or cut off parts of their body in the image. Alex was able to trick the sensor to include most of the people. He would arrange them in a certain way so the sensor would pick them up. Most of the time Alex was able to get a great group photo. What made it easy for Alex was that he could see the image in real-time before taking it. This allowed him to reposition people as needed. He developed quite a knack for positioning people. After the event we acquired a Kinect for Windows. When we connected this version of the Kinect, we found that it worked much better to capture people in a group. It seems this version is better suited. This is probably because this Kinect and Software Development Kit are specifically designed to work together. The Xbox 360 version was designed for the Xbox 360 gaming system.

Variations

One amazing variation would be adding a printer. Placing a printout of an instant camera in front of the printer and aligning where the picture would come out with the tray of the printer would give the impression that a photo came out of the camera. This would be simple to do with a very compact inkjet printer. One could set up a macro that automatically prints the photo taken. Another great variation to this project is to take videos instead of images. The Kinect is capable of adding the green-screen effect to videos. Instead of an "instant" camera, build a movie camera, like the ones used in silent films or perhaps an early television studio camera.

Incorporating the Project

This project can easily be incorporated into any library event that wants to see patrons engage with the library. There is no need for an actual green screen, although the camera can be placed virtually anywhere, it is best to place in where there are not too many object in the background. This project is a great tool for social media. Since the camera is mobile, it can be transported just about anywhere.

Key Points

- The Kinect is a great device that allows images to be captured with a digital backdrop without the use of photo editing software.
- Photo booths that have a "green screen" are more engaging for patrons.
- Photo booths are a great tool for getting people to interact with each other.
- The photo booth/selfie station is completely mobile. This allows libraries to use it at any event. Additionally, it is very customizable for all types of events.
- With the popularity of selfies, people are more comfortable taking candid photos of themselves.
- Social media has made it easier to upload and share images with each other.
- Libraries will benefit from this type of photo booth. Rather than having instant gratification of images, patrons will have to access the library social media site to obtain the pictures. This helps to draw users to the library.

References

- Microsoft Kinect for Windows SDK v1.8: https://www.microsoft.com/en-us/download/details.aspx?id=40278
- Microsoft Kinect for Windows Developer Toolkit v1.8: https://www.microsoft.com/en-us/download/confirmation.aspx?id=40276
- GitHub Kinect-Library-Photo-Booth repository: https://github.com/practical-code-for-librarians/Kinect-Library-Photo-Booth

CHAPTER 7

Library Services Scavenger Hunt

Concept and Flow

⊚ Project Description

AS MENTIONED IN OUR AR SCAVENGER HUNT CHAPTER (chapter 2), scavenger hunts are a common library activity. This project twists the expected approach by providing a map to the actual scavenger hunt stations and adding some interactive escape room–style elements, requiring participants to discover codes and secret messages that will lead them to the next clue. Along the way, signs posted at each station, as well as the stations themselves, help participants learn more about library services of the past and present. This is a highly customizable project, with a lot of potential for tweaks and changes to make it relevant to different libraries and even other settings with different goals.

This project includes seven stations, with the first also serving as the starting point and introduction, where participants receive their maps and instructions. Five of the stations will be described in detail in the subsequent chapters, with instructions on how to create them. Two stations were not so much created as designated, relying on the preexisting functionality of the library website. The flow outlined below indicates how all stations fit together and lead to one another, explains how these two stations using preexisting content can be used for the scavenger hunt, and includes details about the overall narrative of the scavenger hunt.

Figure 7.1. Welcome table to begin the scavenger hunt. *Figure by Lillianna Kiel.*

1. Station 1: Clock
    a. Participants arrive at the welcome/start table. The rules are explained and participants are given a map of the stations, as well as a sheet of paper on which to write the final clue.
    b. The welcome table staff asks the first question, or a sign is posted asking the first question. When participants figure out the answer, they push in the numbers on the clock in the correct order, revealing an LCD screen with their first clue: an author's name.
    c. The clock fits into the narrative by transporting the participants back in time to begin their exploration of library services of the past and present.

2. Station 2: Card Catalog
   a. The card catalog is arranged alphabetically by author's last name. Participants search the name discovered at station 1 to find the correct card, which reveals the name of a book by that author.
   b. The card catalog demonstrates how library resources were organized in the past, and how patrons were required to search for books. It leads to its modern equivalent.
3. Station 3: Catalog Computer
   a. This station simply makes use of an existing catalog computer with a sign nearby tying it to the rest of the scavenger hunt. At this station, participants must search the name of the book they have discovered and make note of the call number to find it on the shelves.
   b. The catalog computer demonstrates how organizing and finding library resources has changed and become digital.
4. Station 4: Locked Book
   a. Participants seek out the book they looked up, finding it by call number on the shelf. Beside it is the next station, a special book locked shut with a keypad on the front. The code to open the book is the first three numbers of the call number. The message inside the book directs participants to the next station and asks them to look up a specific journal article among the library's electronic resources.
   b. The book on the shelf is representative of the library's print resources, once the only type of resources available. It serves to help patrons understand how call numbers work and how physical materials are organized.
5. Station 5: Online Resources
   a. As with station 3, this station makes use of existing resources: the library website and a public-access computer. Participants must search for the journal article using the library's discovery system (the overall search which provides results from many different databases). They are asked to remember the article's publication date as they proceed to the next station.
   b. This station demonstrates how the library has expanded beyond print resources on the shelves to many e-resources accessible online through the website.
6. Station 6: Phone
   a. Participants discover an old landline phone. They must dial a code to hear a message (the publication date of the article they found) in order to hear a message. The correct code plays an audio clip through the phone, providing them with a question to "ask a librarian."
   b. The phone represents how patrons might have contacted a librarian for help in the past, if they could not visit the library in person.
7. Station 7: Bot Chat
   a. This station uses existing resources (a public-access computer) along with created resources (a bot chat system). Patrons use the computer, already loaded to the appropriate website, to "chat" with a librarian: a bot that has been designed to give certain answers in response to specific queries. Upon asking the correct question received from the phone, they are provided with the final clue to write down and turn in at the start table.
   b. Though phones are still a valid option for contacting librarians, the online chat represents newer, digital methods for reaching out for help, including one-on-one chat and email.

Lessons Learned

Although our implementation of this project went well, there were a few areas of unexpected difficulties or that could be improved. The main challenge we encountered was that some people, upon using the stations that involved a computer, would proceed to close the browser or change what the browser had been loaded to. This was especially an issue with station 7, the bot chat. As the bot chat was hosted on a different website, there was no easy way for participants to discover it starting from the library website, so if anyone navigated away from it, this made things tricky for the next person. During our run of the scavenger hunt, we managed this by sending helpers to periodically check the computers, but we would seek out a better solution if running this again.

Having a few helpers check the stations every so often was extremely useful, and is a good recommended practice. Other than keeping the bot chat computer pointed where it should be, our helpers were also able to fix small issues such as participants re-shelving the locked book incorrectly so others couldn't find it.

Another tweak we would make for future implementation of the scavenger hunt would be clarifying some of the language used in our clues and signs. For example, the message on the phone instructed participants to "ask a librarian" the provided question. We intended for people to proceed to the next marked station on the map, discover the "librarian" bot chat, and understand they were being asked to use it. However, some participants' interpretations led them to simply ask the question of the librarian currently staffing the reference desk, who was taken by surprise and not necessarily prepared for this to happen.

Finally, in further developing this project for the future, we would like to explore more ways to increase the accessibility. As our phone clue was audio only, we added an LCD screen with a text transcript for participants who might be deaf or hard of hearing. However, many of our clues relied on sight and reading, and a number relied on participants being able to use a computer or manipulate an object like a keypad. We realize this fell short in making the project accessible to everyone, and we would like to explore alternate methods of providing clues so each person could have an equivalent experience.

Variations

- Change the narrative and overall concept: While the original project employs a narrative of traveling through time to explore library services, this is easy to adapt and change. We mainly conveyed the story of the scavenger hunt and details of the stations with signs posted near each one, so the language on these signs can be altered to fit any context that makes sense for you. The clues and codes provided throughout can also be changed to fit better with the new idea of the scavenger hunt. In our version, we connected stations visually by choosing an image to include at each one (i.e., on the locked book, used as the bot chat's avatar, on station signs). Choosing an appropriate themed image will also contribute to the overall narrative.

  Overhauling the narrative could even make this project work outside a library setting entirely. Many elements (clock, phone, etc.) are not specific to libraries, and those that are, like a card catalog, could be changed to something more generic such as a filing cabinet.

- Remix and separate individual elements: Many of the individual elements that make up the different stations (i.e. locked book, clock with a secret message) can be remixed any way you choose or separated from the overall scavenger hunt idea to be used in different projects. For example, you might be interested in setting up something that leans more heavily toward an escape room, and could incorporate some of the specific projects into this. Some stations could be entirely eliminated if they don't make sense for you, or new and different stations could be added.
- Add challenge: When we implemented the scavenger hunt, our audience was primarily families visiting the library as part of our 50th Anniversary Celebration, held during Friends and Family weekend on our college campus. As a result, we didn't expect participants to be very familiar with how to navigate the library building or website, and we wanted to keep the event fairly short and clear to move through so they could attend other events that day. If you feel your audience might be up for more of a challenge, you might eliminate the station maps and make finding them a part of the game, or find other ways to tweak clues and elements to raise the difficulty level.

Key Points

- This seven-station scavenger hunt incorporates escape room–style elements of finding clues and codes to progress.
- Some stations involved creating special devices or projects, to be detailed in the next chapters, while some took advantage of existing resources.
- This project is highly customizable with a lot of remix potential, and can be adapted to include different narratives, settings, stations, elements, and so on.

Scavenger Hunt
Clock

Project Description

THIS PROJECT IN THE LIBRARY SERVICES SCAVENGER HUNT has participants retrieving a clue from a clock with an LCD display. To access the clue, a participant must enter a four digit-code using the clock-face numbers. The trigger on the clock does not actually rely on a four-digit code. It is only the last digit in the code. Once triggered a trap door will open to reveal the coded message on the LCD display.

Figure 8.1. Scavenger Hunt Clock. *Figure by Juan Denzer.*

⊚ Materials List

- Any wall clock with embossed numbers. The numbers must be detachable from the clock face.
- (2) R3 Uno Arduino boards
- (2) USB charging cables for the R3 Uno boards.
- (12) Push-down button with a ballpoint pen spring (pen springs) https://www .thingiverse.com/thing:1597725
- One 20 × 2 Character LCD Module with I2C Interface
- One SG90 micro servo motor
- One small DIY speaker
- Mini momentary switch button
- One Dfplayer Mini MP3 Player Module for Arduino Voice Module for Arduino
- One micro SD card capable of storing at least ten megabytes of storage for audio
- Jumper wires for Arduino: male to male, male to female, female to female (Approximately eight inches in length per jumper)
- Prototype breadboard
- Duct tape
- Electrical tape
- Masking tape
- Small zip ties
- Foam poster board
- Arduino Uno R3 Case https://www.thingiverse.com/thing:101985 (optional)

⊚ Necessary Equipment

- Both a flat-head and Philips-head screw driver.
- Laptop or PC that can run Arduino IDE software
- Scissors or box-cutter knife
- Hot glue gun
- Electric drill with various drill bit sizes
- Hole saw bits capable of making a hole the size of the 3-D push buttons
- Box cutter knife
- Solder kit
- Multi-meter with continuity mode
- Sharpie
- JB Weld bonding material

⊚ Step-by-Step

1. Begin by building each 3-D printed button and sealing them with bonding material. Make sure the buttons do not stick and that they move freely up and down. Leave at least one button disassembled. This will be the trigger button with the code that a user enters.
2. Lightly trace an outline of all the numbers on the face of the clock. It will be necessary to know the exact location of the numbers.

Figure 8.2. Embossed numbers. *Figure by Juan Denzer.*

3. Next, carefully remove all the numbers on the face of the clock. Be careful not to damage the numbers. Also store them in a safe location.
4. Take a piece of poster board and create an overlay of the clock's face. This will serve as the layer that holds the numbers in place when they are pressed.
5. This step is tricky. The outline numbers on the clock face need to be drawn on the poster board overlay. This can be done by measuring the location of the numbers. It can be done freely by hand. The best approach is to photocopy the clock's face so they can be traced. This might be difficult if the clock is larger than what can be copied on a copier.
6. Cut out all the traced numbers on the overlay. Make sure the number that you removed in step 3 fits snug but can freely move up and down. If they do not move freely, it might be necessary to make the cutouts bigger. Be careful not make them too big.

7. Take the unassembled 3-D button and use it as a template. The larger outer ring will serve as a guide for the holes of each number on the clock. Place the overlay onto the clock face. With the 3-D button outer ring as a guide, center in each number, cut out and trace the circle on the clock face. Do this for each number. Double digits might require removing the overlay and making an estimated circle.

8. When all the circles are drawn on the clock face, begin to cut out the holes for the push buttons. Use a correctly sized hole bit to make the holes. Take all the built push buttons and bond them to the holes on the back of the clock. Be careful not to get boding material on the tops of the button as it might seal them tight. Do not add a push button to the number that is the trigger digit in the code. Test to make sure the buttons are working freely.

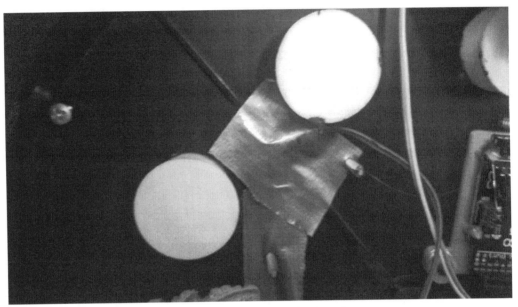

Figure 8.3. 3D push button on back of clock. *Figure by Juan Denzer.*

9. Next, carefully place the numbers onto each corresponding push button and bond them to the top of the button. Check to make sure each number moves freely when pressed.

10. Take the unassembled push button and add the mini momentary switch button. The switch will need two leads that will act as the trigger for the Arduino board. The switch will go inside the button and the wires will come out the back of the 3-D button. Attach the button to the last hole on the clock.

11. This step involves making the trap door for the LCD. Start by finding a good location for the LCD such as above the number six. Also make sure the location does not interfere with the push buttons in the back of the clock. Draw an outline of the LCD face that is slightly large in size. Cut out the trap door and save the cutout. Test to make sure the LCD is visible from the front of the clock. Remember that the LCD will have to be attached a little farther from the clock. This is so the door has room to open and close. Add a small hinge to the door piece and attach it to the back of the clock. Make sure it is secured to the top of the opening. The door should naturally close with the help of gravity.

12. Next add the servo so it can open the trap door. The servo can be attached to an arm that will pull on a string to open the door. The best location for the string

is on the bottom of the trap door. Mount the servo somewhere on the back of the clock so the arm moves freely and pulls to open the door. This will take some adjustments to get it right.

Figure 8.4. Trap door for LCD. *Figure by Juan Denzer.*

13. Mount the LCD to the back of the clock making sure it is aligned with trap door opening and clears the door.
14. The code and wiring is available from a special GitHub repository specifically written for this book. Download the Arduino source code and upload it to the board. Test to make sure the system is working correctly.
15. Finally, build a support for the clock. Since each clock is different, the kind of stand you make is up to the maker.

Lessons Learned

There was so much to learn from this project. It helped to strengthen our maker building skills. This included finding the best 3-D printed spring-loaded push buttons. We tried all types of setups before settling on the spring-loaded push button design. How the clue was going to be delivered also proved to be a challenge. The goal was to have a clockface that appeared to be untouched. This required some way of revealing an LCD display to the user. We decided on making some sort of sliding door. This involved using a track that would allow the door to slide in one direction to open and then close in the opposite direction. The end result was not as expected. The door would not fully open or close. This was mostly due to the calibration of the servo in the code. Instead a simpler approach was taken. A spring-loaded trap door was designed. This removed the need for precise movements for opening and closing the door. All that was needed was a way to open the door in one direction and gravity took care of closing the door.

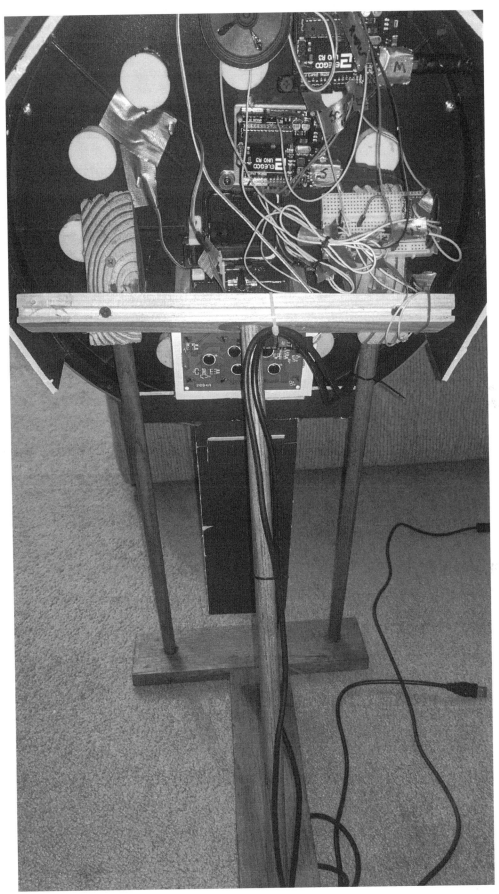

Figure 8.5. Back of clock. *Figure by Juan Denzer.*

◎ Variations

This project is the most complex of all the projects. So much planning and testing was done throughout the process. The variations in the project will come from all the ideas that each maker will come up with on their own. One variation that would have been added if there was more time was a moving clock pendulum. Another variation is to replace the LCD trap door with a pocket. The pocket can be used to dispense a written note or key. The clock could also play an audio clue instead of a written clue. One other variation is to add a glass door to the front face of the clock with a key. This gives it a more mysterious feel when a user is about to interact with the clock.

◎ References

- GitHub Arduino-Interactive-clock repository: https://github.com/practical-code -for-librarians/Arduino-Clock-Puzzle
- Arduino IDE: https://www.arduino.cc/en/main/software

CHAPTER 9

Scavenger Hunt
Card Catalog

IN THIS CHAPTER

▷ Project Description

▷ Materials List

▷ Necessary Equipment

▷ Step-by-Step

▷ Lessons Learned

▷ Variations

⊚ Project Description

AS PART OF THE LIBRARY SERVICES SCAVENGER HUNT, participants come across an old card catalog filled with cards arranged alphabetically by author's last name. One of the cards is a specially prepared custom card containing a clue and some information about how to proceed to the next station. The card catalog represents the past of organizing and searching for library resources.

Figure 9.1. The project can be set up in any size card catalog. *Figure by Lillianna Kiel.*

🌀 Materials List

- Card catalog of any size (smaller with fewer drawers is preferable as it will mean less work to prepare)
- Cards to fill drawers (If your library already has old catalog cards lying around, these are ideal. If not, use index cards or something similar.)

⊚ Necessary Equipment

- None

⊚ Step-by-Step

1. If you start with blank cards, fill them in with information. They don't need to mimic catalog cards perfectly; simply writing an author's name and a book title is sufficient.
2. Prepare one special card with the clue: the author's name received from the previous station and the name of the book participants will have to search at the next station. If you're using any visuals to tie clues together, such as a special image, you can put it on this card, as well. You may also choose to include information about how to proceed at the next station (i.e., "At station three, search for the name of this book to continue").

McCrobie, Mike.
    Our Oswego: memories of growing up & growing old in the port city of central New York, By Mike McCrobie; illustrated by Melissa (Francisco) Martin ... New York, Mike McCrobie, 2014.
    151 p.   23 cm.

Micro
AFS
McC

Figure 9.2. Example of a card prepared for the scavenger hunt. *Figure by Sharona Ginsberg.*

3. Arrange the cards in the drawers of the card catalog by author's last name. It's not necessary to fill every drawer completely, or even to fill every drawer. Include however many cards seems appropriate, and enough to conceal the specially prepared card.
4. Create a sign to mark the station and provide any instructions or pieces of the narrative you would like.

Figure 9.3. Card catalog station set up with a sign. *Figure by Lillianna Kiel.*

◉ Lessons Learned

Some card catalogs have rods for each drawer, and cards have holes punched in the bottom to slide onto these rods. If you are able to use drawers like this, it's ideal, as participants cannot remove the special clue card and/or accidentally put it back in the wrong location. If your card catalog doesn't have these rods, make sure to have a helper periodically check the station to keep things in order.

Unless learning more about how to use the online catalog is part of the challenge of the scavenger hunt, avoid creating confusion for participants and choose a book that is relatively easy to find with a unique title. If desired, you can tie the book into the theme or narrative of your scavenger hunt in some way.

⊚ Variations

As mentioned in chapter 7, the scavenger hunt is very customizable and you can alter the narrative in any way you'd like. As such, the content of the cards doesn't need to be books and authors, but can be anything that fits. Cards can be arranged in any order that makes sense, but be sure to let participants know how they should be searching.

If running the scavenger hunt outside a library setting without a library-related narrative—or if you simply can't find an old card catalog to use—switch out the catalog for something similar, like a filing cabinet, a series of boxes, and so on. Be creative in finding materials that can work and seem appropriate for your personalized approach. The key to the idea is that participants are searching for a clue and learning something about a system of organization along the way.

Scavenger Hunt

Locked Book

─── **IN THIS CHAPTER** ───

▷ Project Description

▷ Materials List

▷ Necessary Equipment

▷ Step-by-Step

▷ Lessons Learned

▷ Variations

Project Description

THIS PROJECT IN THE LIBRARY SERVICES SCAVENGER HUNT has participants retrieving a clue from a book with an electronic lock mechanism. To access the clue, a participant must enter a four-digit code into a keypad. This will trigger a solenoid which will release a latch and the book can be opened. The clue is on the first page of the book.

Figure 10.1.   Scavenger Hunt Locked book. *Figure by Juan Denzer.*

Ⓖ Materials List

- Any 9" × 6" × 2" or larger hardcover book, preferably one that is used or discarded and has a black cover
- One Arduino Uno Board or equivalent that uses a USB type port for power
- 5V USB slim power back
- One 3 × 4 phone-style Matrix Keypad (Adafruit Part #1842)
- One Lock-style Solenoid – 12VDC (Adafruit Part #1512)
- 5V relay module for Arduino ARM PIC AVR MCU 5V Indicator Light LED 1 channel relay module
- Two 9V battery clip connector, T Type
- Jumper wires for Arduino: male to male, male to female, female to female (Approximately eight inches in length per jumper)
- 3-D printed 9V battery holder https://www.thingiverse.com/thing:2953775 (optional)
- Duct tape
- Various small screws
- Small piece of wood, about 1" × 1" × 7"
- 5" × 8" × ¼" clear acrylic Plexiglas
- Electrical tape
- Small zip ties
- Wood or machine screws of various lengths
- Velcro-type strips
- Mod Podge
- Strong bonding adhesive

🌀 Necessary Equipment

- Both a flat-head and Philips-head screwdriver
- Laptop or PC that can run Arduino IDE software https://www.arduino.cc/en/main/software
- Box cutter knife
- Wire strippers
- Electric drill with various drill bit sizes
- Multi-meter with continuity mode
- Pencil
- Sharpie
- Handheld vacuum
- Pair of ratcheting bar clamps/spreaders
- Wooden plank, larger than the chosen book
- Oscillating multi-tool (optional)

🌀 Step-by-Step

1. Begin by measuring and drawing a rectangle on top of the first page of the book. The rectangle should be approximately one inch from all sides. The goal is to have a cutout that is large enough to fit all the electronic components.

2. Use a box cutter knife or an oscillating multi-tool to cut out the rectangle. Make sure that the cuts are square. Take your time so that you do not cut on an angle. It is important that the rectangle is as square as possible. Use a pair of ratcheting bar clamp/spreaders to keep the book stable. This will also help keep the pages from slipping. Cut deep enough so that all the main components will fit easily in the book. This includes the solenoid which will be attached to the inside cover on the book. The solenoid should also have room to fit inside the book.

3. Once the rectangle cutout is done, clean up the inside as much as possible. Blow out the opening and carefully use a handheld vacuum to clear out debris. Avoid sucking up pages as the vacuum can tear them out. Double check to make sure all the components fit inside.

4. Next, use Mod Podge to seal the book. Start by spreading the glue in between some pages of the book. Do not put any glue on the first page or the inside cover of the book. Once the glue is in between the pages, place a wooden plank and use a pair of ratcheting bar clamp/spreaders to secure the book. Use a few books to support the inside cover. The cover should be parallel to the inside of the book. You want to make sure the spine of the book is not stressed causing the pages to slide. Then continue to add more glue to the outside of the book. Allow the book to dry. Then add a second coat of glue. Let the entire book dry. Once dry, take off the wooden plank and apply glue the inside of the cutout. Also apply glue to the top page of the book as well as the inside spine.

5. Take a sheet of clear acrylic Plexiglas and place it over the book cutout. Measure about a ¼" border larger than the book cutout. The Plexiglas will serve as a cover to protect the components; it will also serve as the cover that holds clues or instructions in a scavenger hunt. Trim the Plexiglas to the measurements in this step. Center the sheet over the cutout and draw an outline with a pencil. Using

Figure 10.2. Hollowed out book. *Figure by Juan Denzer.*

the box cutter carve out about ¼" deep along the drawn outline. The Plexiglas should lay flush with the top few pages of the book. The cover should be flat when the book is closed.

6. The next step is to secure the keypad to the front cover. Center the keypad and lightly press it into the cover. The pins from the keypad should make a slight mark. Use the marks as a guide to cut out a rectangular hole. The hole should be wide enough for the pins to pass through the cover. Use four tiny screws to secure the keypad to the cover. If screws are unavailable, then use a strong adhesive.

7. Take a small piece of wood to create a brace that will allow the solenoid to latch on. Make sure the wood is flush with the cutout. Use a strong adhesive to bond the wood to the right inside of the rectangular cutout.

8. Next will be to add the solenoid. This step may take a lot of positioning and repositioning of the solenoid to get it to fit correctly. The best approach is to use duct tape to temporarily hold the solenoid in place while marking the position. This will allow you to make adjustments before permanently fixing the solenoid. Start by closing the cover, and draw a small line where the edge of the wood in the cutout aligns the cover. This will be the baseline for where the solenoid will be placed. Center the solenoid on the inside cover of the book. It should be opposite of the keypad; this will help keep the locked book balanced. Make sure the latch is facing to the left of the cover. Align the metal edge of the solenoid where the latch sticks out to the drawn line on the cover. Create a shim out of wood or plastic to serve as a strong base for the solenoid. This is necessary because the cover is not strong enough to support screws. Make sure the shim is slightly larger than the solenoid. Secure the solenoid to the shim using small wood screws. Remember to pre-drill holes into the shim to avoid splitting the shim.

9. This next step involves positioning the solenoid so that the cover will close nicely. Someone using the locked book should be able to close the book without having to force it closed. They should not be able to shift the cover that causes the book to unlock either. Start by closing the cover and make sure the solenoid does not hit the wood inside the book. It should be able to clear the edge while still being close to the wood. If there is too much distance between the solenoid and the wood, the latch will not be secure. This may take a lot of repositioning; adjust as needed. Once the solenoid is in the proper position, mark where the latch touches the wood. You will need to carve out a hole so the latch can slide easily when the cover is closed. Try to make the hole as square as possible. This will make a more secured fit. Make sure the latch is snug inside the hole. Test the make sure the latch is secured well and the locking of the book does not feel loose. If the latch is not secured and it feels as if it can be easily pried open, you will need to add a latching piece. Take a small piece or thin metal or plastic, use the extra scraps from the Plexiglas. Use this piece to add better latching support for the solenoid. Secure it using either some wood screws or a strong adhesive. Test the latching setup to make sure it is secure and working properly. When testing, it might be necessary to force the book open to get it open. Be careful when prying it open. Avoid doing it too much. Use a tiny screwdriver to pop it open. Once you are confident that the latch is working well, secure the shimmed solenoid to the inside cover using a strong adhesive.

10. Next, you will want to lay out the components so that wires can be measured and properly placed inside the book. It is important to lay out the components in such a way that they are easily accessible for making connection, replacement, and charging or changing the batteries. Start with the 5V power bank. Place it in a corner with the ports toward the inside of the book. Make sure that the port is easy to access with a USB power cable. It might be necessary to add shims made out of foam or poster board. Some power banks might be so thin that it makes it hard to plug in a USB cable when flat. Then secure the power bank to the inside bottom of the book with Velcro strips. Next, secure the Arduino board onto the flat power bank using Velcro strips. The power port on the Arduino should be generally aligned with the ports on the power bank. Use the shortest USB power cord to connect the power bank and Arduino. The less clutter the better. Find a good location for the 5v Relay Module. The best place is adjacent

to the book spine, since it will connect to the solenoid. Secure it using two wood screws. Avoid using adhesives or Velcro. Place the two 9V batteries inside the book next to the relay. If you are using the optional 3-D printed holder, secure it to the inside. Make sure the batteries do not stick out. If you are not using a holder, use Velcro to secure them inside.

11. Wiring all the components in this step is not difficult. Begin with the relay which will be used to trigger the solenoid. The solenoid needs more than 9V of power to trigger it, this is why two 9V batteries are used. They will need to be wired in series to create 18V. Take two 9V battery clip connectors and connect the negative wire (-) of one connector to the red wire (+) of the other connector and secure the end with electrical tape. Take a red male pin jumper wire and cut and strip one end. Connect the stripped end to the free red wire (+) from the two 9V battery clip connector and seal them with electrical tape. Quickly test the solenoid with the connector. Plug a 9V battery in each clip connector. Then insert the male pin which is the red wire (+) into the positive female end on the solenoid. Take the free black wire (-) and touch the negative female end on the solenoid. The solenoid should trigger the latch pin. Do not hold it to the negative female end on the solenoid for more than a few seconds. Cut and strip a black male pin jumper wire to make the negative (-) connector for the solenoid to relay. Now make the connections for the solenoid to relay. Look at the relay, there should be three screw type connections: normally open (NO), COM, and normally closed (NC). Take the free black wire (-) from the 9V battery clip connector and insert it into the normally open (NO). Take the stripped black male pin jumper wire and connect it to the COM. Insert the male end into the female negative (-) end of the solenoid. Take the red male pin jumper end and insert it into the female positive (+) end of the solenoid. Use electrical tape to secure the jumper connections. Run the wires along the inside cover of the book and secure them with duct tape. Now it is time to connect the wires that will power the relay and connect to the Arduino board. Take three male-to-female jumper wires that are long enough to reach the relay and Arduino board. Mark each wire as follows: neg (-), pos (+), and S. Connect each female to the corresponding male pins on the relay.

12. This next step will connect the relay and keypad to the Arduino board. Connect the neg (-) male jumper pin from the relay to GND on the Arduino. Connect the pos (+) male jumper pin from the relay to 5V on the Arduino. Connect the S male jumper pin from the relay to pin 10 on the Arduino. Take seven male-to-female jumper wires that are long enough to reach the keypad pins and Arduino board. Use separate colored wires and number them two through eight. If using the same colored wires, make sure to clearly label them with masking tape. Then take the female ends of the wires and connect them to the keypad pins. Starting from the left, skip the first pin. Connect 2 through 8 in order. You should have a total of seven wires connected. The pins used will be digital pins 2 through 8 on the Arduino board. The pin will be matched in reverse order from step 7. So keypad pin 2 will match with analog pin 8, keypad pin 3 with analog pin 7, keypad pin 4 with analog pin 6, and so on. Secure the wire with zip ties and use duct tape to attach them to the inside of the book cover.

13. Once all the wiring is done, it is time to upload the code to the Arduino. The code is available from a special GitHub repository specifically written for this

book. Download the Arduino source code and upload it to the board. Test to make sure the system is working correctly. Connect the Arduino USB power to the power bank and plug in the two 9V batteries. Test the system by pressing "#" and the digit code set in the source code on the keypad. The solenoid latch should retract for a second then release.

14. Next, prepare the Plexiglas cover. It will need a cutout so the solenoid and keypad wiring can easily pass through when the cover is opened and closed. Place the Plexiglas onto the larger cutout. Mark an estimate where the keypad pins and solenoid make contact and make a cutout. It might be necessary to trim more for the opening as is it tricky to estimate. Remember that the solenoid pin has been taped down, take that into account in your estimates. Once the cutout is complete, the Plexiglas will need to be secured. It should not be a permanent solution. The Plexiglas should be removable in a way where users cannot easily take it off. This is done by using wood screws that are about 1" in length. Mark the four corners of the Plexiglas with a dot. They should be placed in a location where they are not too close to the edge and will make contact with the book. Carefully drill the four holes into the Plexiglas. They should be larger enough to where the screws will pass through easily. Do not make them too large. Take your time when drilling, do not force the drill. This will cause the Plexiglas to split.

15. Finally, add labels to the locked book. This will include labeling the spine, hint for unlocking, and the clue inside. It is best not to use permanent tape or

Figure 10.3. Clear Plexiglas cover.
Figure by Juan Denzer.

adhesives. This project is intended to be used for different types of events or scavenger hunts. When adding text, make sure it is readable. Instructions on how to use the book are important as well. Even something as simple as putting in a code is not clear to everyone.

Lessons Learned

One of the best things about working on projects such as this one, you develop this knack for improving your skills. So much trial and error helps us come up with better solutions. One example includes placing the solenoid on the inside of this book. This not only makes the book more polished, but it also makes it more durable for the future. Another lesson that was learned was choosing better hardware. We found that it might have been easier to a use a flat keypad that uses a ribbon connector. It allows for the book to easily be hidden in the stacks. It also makes it easier to work with. We also learned about the durability of the locked book. Most of these projects take some care in storing them. It is important to make sure they last for reuse. Powering the locked book was something that we learned could be better implemented. The challenge for this project was powering the solenoid. This required two 9V batteries which is not typical of the common 5V power sources for the other projects. One lesson we learned was not to use permanent tape and adhesive for the clues. It wasn't until after creating the locked book for the scavenger hunt that we realized the project could be used for other events. When working on these types of projects it is best to think of how they can be reused in the future.

Variations

One variation for the locked book includes creating a charging port for the battery packs. A USB port can easily be carved out on the text block of the book. This can be done using a modified USB cable. This will make it easier to recharge the locked book because it will not require the removal of the Plexiglas to access the battery pack. The same can be done for the 9V batteries, although 9V rechargeable batteries might require a little more planning. Another variation might include adding low-powered LEDs. LEDs are easy to add and give the added surprise of accomplishment. A roller type toggle switch can be used to trigger the LEDs. Sound is another great variation that can be added. Since the project uses an Arduino board, adding a simple speaker to play a sound is easy. The locked book is not only limited to relying on written clues. It can also be designed to hold other items for a scavenger hunt. This could be things like a USB thumb drive, keys, tokens, business cards, and so on. This might require a larger book, so a slot can be carved out for such items. The project in chapters 8 and 11 uses a LCD to display the clue. This can also be added to this project. The code in those chapters can be used to add a LCD to the locked book. This will also make it easier to change the clues, rather than having to relabel the inside. It also adds a nice "cool" factor.

References

- GitHub Arduino-Book-Safe repository: https://github.com/practical-code-for-librarians/Arduino-Book-Safe

Scavenger Hunt

Phone

 Project Description

THIS PROJECT IN THE LIBRARY SERVICES SCAVENGER HUNT has participants retrieving a clue from an old touch-tone phone. To access the clue, a participant must enter a four-digit code. The phone will then play a prerecorded message with the clue. If any other four-digit code is entered, a prerecorded "wrong number" message will be played. The phone has the effect of a dial tone to give it that authentic old phone experience. The phone is also equipped with a small LCD screen for those who are hearing impaired.

Figure 11.1. Scavenger Hunt Arduino powered phone. *Figure by Juan Denzer.*

🌀 Materials List

- Any square-type keypad phone with a handheld receiver. Make sure it is not the receiver with the keypad built in. Those phones may not be large enough to accommodate the electronic modifications. Make sure the hand-receiver is intact.
- One USB cable of at least 2–3 feet. One end must be of Type-A, this is the male end that is rectangle and about ½" is width. The other end is not important as it is not needed for this project.
- One 5V USB Type-A charger or USB chargeable battery pack
- One Arduino Mega 2560 board
- One Serial MP3 player board by Catalex
- One micro SD card capable of storing at least ten megabytes for audio recordings
- One 20 × 2 Character LCD Module with I2C Interface

- One 3 × 4 Phone-style Matrix Keypad (Adafruit Part #1842)
- Jumper wires for Arduino: male to male, male to female, female to female (Approximately eight inches in length per jumper)
- One TS or TRS 3.5mm audio cable with a minimum of six inches (basic mean)
- Small prototype breadboard
- Duct tape
- Electrical tape
- Masking tape
- Small zip ties
- Foam poster-board
- 3-D printed Arduino Mega 2560 full bottom cover plate with mounting screws https://www.thingiverse.com/thing:618520 (optional)
- 3-D printed Catalex/YX5300 (Serial UART MP3 Module) Mount https://www.thingiverse.com/thing:2996112 (optional)

⊚ Necessary Equipment

- Both a flat-head and Philips-head screw driver
- Laptop or PC that can run Arduino IDE software https://www.arduino.cc/en/main/software
- Scissors or box cutter knife
- Hot glue gun
- Wire strippers
- Soldering kit
- Electric drill with various drill bit sizes
- Multi-meter with continuity mode
- Sharpie

⊚ Step-by-Step

1. Begin by removing all unneeded internal parts of the phone. This is done so that there is plenty of room for the new electronic components. Remove the internal ringer, it is usually two cup-shaped bells. When cutting the wires, leave enough length so they can be used later. This is especially important for the jack where the handset is connected. Next remove the touch keypad. Finally, remove the handset rocker switch and set it aside. It will be used later in the project. Do not discard it.

2. Next, prepare the USB Type-A cable so that it can be used to power the phone. Cut off the non Type-A end of the USB cable and strip away the sheathing to expose the internal wires. The cable will have either two or four wires. If it has only two wires, then the cable is for power only. This makes it easier to identify the wires. The VCC or +5V is indicated by a red wire. The GND also known as the ground wire is black. If you have four wires, then you are using a cable that is both power and data. The data wires are not used in the project. You can ignore them or cut them off at the stump. Once you have identified the VCC and GND wire, use the wire stripper to expose the wire ends and label them with masking tape.

3. Take the wired end of the USB cable and pass it from the outside of the phone shell and in, this will keep it looking clean. It is recommended you pass

it through the line-in jack on the phone. It might be necessary to drill a hole through the jack or create a new hole. Feed the end so it reaches the other side of the phone. Use a glue gun to apply glue on the inside where the cable enters. This will protect the cable from damage if pulled on when in use.

4. Now take the rocker switch that you previously set aside in step one. The USB cable will be wired to the switch which will be how the phone is activated. The switch will also act as the on/off trigger for the phone. This allows the phone to be off when the handset is in the cradle. When the handset is lifted, the system will power on and a dial tone is heard, just like an old-fashioned phone. Take the switch and determine which leads from the switch are continuous when normally closed. Normally open means the switch will make a circuit when it is in a normal position. For the phone, that means the handset is not in the cradle. Take a multimeter and set it to continuity mode. Probe the pins on the back of the switch until you get continuity. Once you determine continuity, test that the circuit will be open when you push on the switch. If the circuit is continuous, then you have found the leads. Mark them with a sharpie. Next prepare the soldering kit so the USB cable can be added to the switch. Take the ground wire from the USB cable and solder it to one of the marked leads on the switch. Take a jumper wire with a male end, preferably a black wire, cut off the non-male end and solder it to the ground wire on the USB cable. Take another jumper wire with a male end, preferably a red wire, cut off the non-male end and solder it to the VCC wire on the USB cable. Finally, test the USB cable and switch. Take the ground lead-pin and insert it into the GND pin on the Arduino board. The VCC lead-pin will be inserted into the VIN pin on the Arduino board. Plug the USB cable into the USB charger to power the board. The board should power on and show lighted LEDs. Push and hold the switch, the board should be off. Release again to make sure it turns on. If the switch is not working, check the connections. If the switch is acting in reverse, check the work by going over this step. Finally, place the switch back in the original position before you removed it. Make sure it is functioning correctly when the handset is placed and removed from the cradle. This will require partially putting the phone case back together.

5. Next, prepare the 3.5mm audio cable so it can be connected to the phone handset. Strip away the sheathing to expose the bare wires on the non-male side of the cable. Identify the ground wire, this will commonly be the black wire. If you do not have a black wire, use the multimeter to test which wire is ground. To do this, set the meter to continuity mode. Take one probe on the meter and touch the base of the 3.5mm plug. Touch the other meter probe to each bare wire on the audio cable. Once you find continuous connection, that is the ground wire. The other wire(s) will be either the mono or left and right wire. Only the ground and one other wire is needed. Locate the black, yellow, red, and green wires that are connected to the phone's headset jack socket. Strip away and expose the red and green wire. These are the speaker wire of the handset. Connect the ground wire from the audio cable to the red wire. Connect the other audio wire to the green wire. Secure the wire connections with electrical tape. Test the audio connection. Plug the 3.5mm jack into an external audio device that plays sound, such as a laptop or smartphone. Connect the phone's handset into the handset jack. Play a sound with the external audio device. Sound should be heard through the

phone's handset. If you do not hear sound playing, check your connections and go through step 5 again.

6. This step will involve preparing the micro SD card so it can be used in the Serial mp3 player board. Format the SD card so that it is completely empty. SD cards that have other files might interfere with playback. Create three separate folders on the SD card labeled: 01, 02, and 03. Each folder will contain one mp3 recorded file with the folder name followed by "xxx." So folder 01 will have a file called 01xxx.mp3. Next create three custom recordings. The first (01xxx.mp3) will be the clue used when someone enter the correct number in the phone. The second (02xxx.mp3) is the wrong number message. The third (03xxx.mp3) is for the dial tone sound. This file should be a thirty-second looping of classic phone dial tone. Use any external program to create the sounds and make sure they are in mp3 format. Audacity is an excellent free application that can be used to created and convert mp3 audio files. Make sure the audio message is short and simple. Also avoid using high sampling rates that make the files large. The audio files should be no larger than 2mb. Audio files that are larger, such as those in 10mb or more, might have unexpected playback. Once the mp3 files are created, copy each file into its corresponding folder. Make sure that only one file is placed in each folder.

7. Next, prepare the 3 × 4 Phone-style Matrix Keypad. Take the original bezel on the phone and place it over the keypad. The bezel opening might be smaller or larger that the keypad. If it is smaller, the bezel will need to be cut to accommodate the keypad. If it is larger, create an inner bezel made out of foam board or heavy card-stock paper. This will help fill any gaps between the original bezel. Secure the keypad to the bezel with duct tape. Now take seven male-to-female jumper wires. Use separate colored wires and number them two through eight. If using the same colored wires, make sure to clearly label them with masking tape. Then take the female ends of the wires and connect them to the keypad pins. Starting from the left, skip the first pin. Connect 2 through 8 in order. You should have a total of seven wires connected. Once the keypad is wired and secured to the bezel, place it back into the phone shell. The keypad is ready and will be wired to the Arduino board in a later step.

8. Take the micro SD card with the recorded audio files and insert it in to the Serial MP3 player board. Find a flat spot inside the phone where the board can be placed and secured with duct tape. Avoid attaching it to the phone shell as this makes it hard to manage the wires as well as putting the phone back together. If you are using the optional 3-D printed case for the board, place it into the board and secure the case to the phone with a strong adhesive such as bonding epoxy. Also the 3-D printed case is designed so that the micro SD card can be easily removed. Try making or use an existing opening in the bottom of the phone when placing the Serial MP3 player board. Position it in such a way that will give you access to the micro SD card from the bottom. This is very useful in making the project upgradable. This will allow you to remove the card without having to take apart the phone when you want to change the recordings. Insert the 3.5mm end of the audio cable in the board. Next take four male-to-female jumper wires and label them GND, VCC, TX, and RX. Connect them to the J2 connector in the board. The board should be clearly labeled GND, VCC, TX, and RX. If it is not labeled well, consult the specifications for the board. Use either zip ties or electrical tape to bundle the wires together. Do not roll them

up and tie them together as the full length of the wires are needed to connect to the main Arduino board.

9. Now prewire the LCD module. Take four male-to-female jumper wires and label them GND, VCC, SDA, and SLA. Connect them to the I2C board on the module. The board should be clearly labeled GND, VCC, SDA, and SLA. If it is not labeled well, consult the specifications for the board. Use either zip ties or electrical tape to bundle the wires together as you did in the previous step. The LCD is placed outside the phone. Find or drill a hole on the bottom of the phone so the wires can be passed through to the inside

10. The next step involves securing the Arduino Mega 2560 Board inside of the base of the phone and wiring together power to all the boards. Locate a comfortable spot for the board. The best location is toward the front underneath the keypad. If you are not using a 3-D printed case, then cut out a piece of foam board the size of the Arduino. Place it under the board. This is done to ensure you don't short out the board when placing it flat on the metal base of the phone. Next secure the board. The best way to secure the board is to use metal screws. The board has predrilled holes that allow metal screws. It might be necessary to drill holes into the phone base in order to secure the board. Be careful not to make the holes larger than the screw. Now take a small breadboard and separate the +/- section. This will give you a +/- and breadboard. Use this to connect the main power cable that will power the Arduino board, Serial to MP3 player board, and the LCD module. Take the VCC lead-pin from step 4, this should be a red wire and insert it into the + side of the breadboard. Take the GND lead-pin and insert it into the − side of the breadboard. The system is now ready to be powered up the other two boards and LCD module. Start with the Serial MP3 player board. Connect the VCC male pin into the + side and the GND male pin into the − side of the breadboard. Wire the VCC and GND of the LCD module the same way as the Serial MP3 player board. Finally, power the Arduino board. Use two male-to-male jumper wires, one for VCC and the other for GND. Insert the VCC into the + side of the breadboard and the other end into the VIN pin on the Arduino. Insert the GND into the − side of the breadboard and the other end into the GND pin on the Arduino which is located right next to the VIN. Once all the power connections are in place, test the system. Connect the USB cable to the USB charger plug in the charger. The LEDs on the Arduino should light up as well as an LED on the Serial MP3 player board. The LCD module display should also be lit up. If the LCD is hard to see, adjust the brightness with the potentiometer on the back of the LCD.

11. The next step involves making all the data connection to the Arduino. Start with the LCD and Serial to MP3 player board. These are the easiest because they only involve two wires each and practically have a one-to-one connection. The SDA wire from the LCD should be connected to the SDA (pin 20) on the Arduino. The SCL wire will connect to the SCL (pin 21). For the Serial to MP3 player board, take the RX and connect it to the TX3 digital Pin 14 on the Arduino. The TX wire will connect to RX3 digital pin 15. *Note: it may seem as if TX3 should be connected to TX and RX3 to RX. The wiring is correct based on the code that is written.* Finally, the keypad will be wired to the Arduino. The pins used will be analog pins 2 through 8 on the Arduino board. The pins will be matched in reverse order from step 7. So keypad pin 2 will match with analog pin 8, keypad pin 3 with analog pin 7, keypad pin 4 with analog pin 6, and so on.

12. Once all the wiring is done, it is time to upload the code to the Arduino. The code is available from a special GitHub repository specifically written for this book. Download the Arduino source code and upload it to the board. Test to make sure the system is working correctly.

13. The last step is to put the phone back together and secure the LCD to the front of the phone.

Lessons Learned

Not all touch-tone phones are built the same. Some may have screws that make them easy to take apart. Others might be glued together which make is a little harder to take apart. Proper care must be taken so that the phone casing is not damaged. Other challenges include wiring. Not every phone, USB cable, or audio cable will follow the same color standards that are listed in the steps. This is why it is important to know how to use a multimeter, so that you can identify specific wires if needed.

Another lesson learned was the realization that not everything can be repurposed. Sometimes it is easier and cheaper to purchase a component. A good example of this was the keypad that came with the phone. Initially the goal was to use the existing keypad. This not only made sense with costs, it also looked more polished, as we would not have had to make a bezel for the added keypad. What we found is that there is no standard matrix for the keypad. This was a challenge because it became a matter of trial and error determine the matrix. This was not only frustrating, but also time consuming. The original keypad was also wired to very thin wires that easily broke off when testing. In the end we determined that the original keypad was no longer practical. It was more ideal to buy a separate keypad.

Variations

Although this project is part of the overall scavenger hunt, it does not have to be exclusively used for scavenger hunts. This setup could be used as a standalone prop to promote a specific event. Or maybe it can be included as part of a library exhibit. Patrons seem to enjoy interacting with displays rather than just looking at them. There are those who might be drawn in with curiosity, while others are drawn in out of nostalgia.

As you develop your maker skills and become comfortable with the technology, you can add variation to the phone. One variation could include having users push buttons to interact with the phone, similar to how automated systems work for support calls. You might even try to use an old-style rotary phone. This is more challenging as it uses electronic pulses to register the numbers. Another fun variation is to add LED lights that give the phone a glowing effect when in use or even when not in use. This is a great way to draw attention to the phone. Users might be intrigued by a glowing phone that will draw their curiosity.

References

- GitHub Arduino-Interactive-Phone repository: https://github.com/practical-code -for-librarians/Arduino-Interactive-Phone

CHAPTER 12

Scavenger Hunt

Bot Chat

IN THIS CHAPTER

▷ Project Description

▷ Materials List

▷ Necessary Equipment

▷ Step-by-Step

▷ Lessons Learned

▷ Variations

Project Description

IN THIS STAGE OF THE LIBRARY SERVICES SCAVENGER HUNT, participants use a public-access computer to speak with a bot acting as a "librarian." They must ask the bot a specific question, received at the last scavenger hunt station, in order to trigger the correct response that provides the final clue. The bot can have as many other triggers for responses as you wish.

When this project was first created, we used an online tool called Botkit, which allowed for the creation and hosting of a bot, as well as editing through a fairly simple interactive interface, Botkit Studio. It eliminated the need for understanding the complexities of how to program a bot or how to code, and made the project fairly quick to put together. Unfortunately, Botkit Studio is no longer an option, and has been replaced by a somewhat more complicated tool called Botkit CMS. As a result, this chapter describes how to create this project using a similar online tool called SnatchBot, which also does not require knowledge of coding or AI.

Figure 12.1. The librarian bot incorporated into the scavenger hunt. *Figure by Lillianna Kiel.*

🌀 Materials List

- None

🌀 Necessary Equipment

- Computer with access to the internet (for setup of the bot)
- A internet-enabled computer station participants can easily access

🌀 Step-by-Step

1. Visit https://snatchbot.me/ and create a free account. After registering, you will be able to log in and access the Dashboard.
2. In the menu on the left, select "My Bots," then click the "Create Bot" button on the top of the window. Give your bot a name that fits into the narrative of your scavenger hunt (i.e., Ask a Librarian), a description, set a language, and upload a picture to represent the bot. (Note: If you're using an image to visually tie together different scavenger hunt stations, this would be a good place to add it.) Click "Create."
3. You will find yourself in the bot editing interface. Click the button for "Add new interaction/plugin." Select the interaction type Bot Statement and name the interaction.

4. Your first interaction will be the first thing the bot does upon being activated—in other words, without needing any interaction from a participant. This can serve as a welcome message and provide any instructions you want to pass along to participants on how to proceed. On the right side of the screen, click on the "Bot Message" field and type in your content.

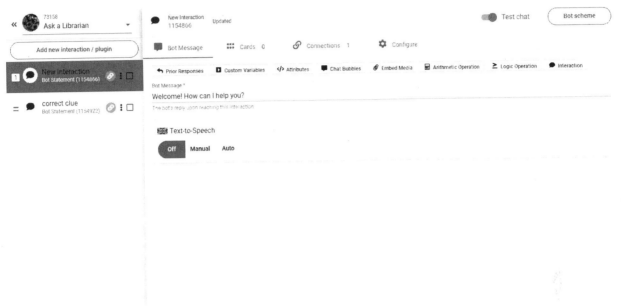

Figure 12.2. The editing interface for bot interactions. *Screenshot of SnatchBot interface from snatchbot.me.*

5. Click the "Add new interaction/plugin" button again and add another Bot Statement. This will be your first response triggered by input. In the "Bot Message" field, type how you would like the bot to respond when the correct question is asked.

6. Return to the first interaction you created. A little above the Bot Message field, there is a horizontal menu. Click over to Connections and scroll to the bottom. Click "Simple Connection." You will be presented with an "If then go to" statement below it. Click this to proceed.

    In the first drop-down menu, select "Response to this interaction" and in the second choose either "exactly matches" or "contains all of." In the keywords field, type your correct question/clue and hit enter or the + button. When the editor asks if it should find synonyms, click cancel. If you want to add variations of the question to allow for common typos or errors, you can do so in this keywords field. Finally, in the last drop-down menu, select the name of the interaction you just created with the response to the question.

    Your connection should look something like this: If [Response to this interaction] [exactly matches] [the correct question/clue participants should ask] then go to [final clue interaction].

7. You may also choose to set up a fallback option (recommended). This will tell the bot what to do if a participant types something that doesn't match the connection you set up. The fallback settings are above the "Simple Connection" button. Create another Bot Statement interaction and you will find it available here on this drop-down list. This statement may be something prompting the participant further or simply stating that the bot does not understand.

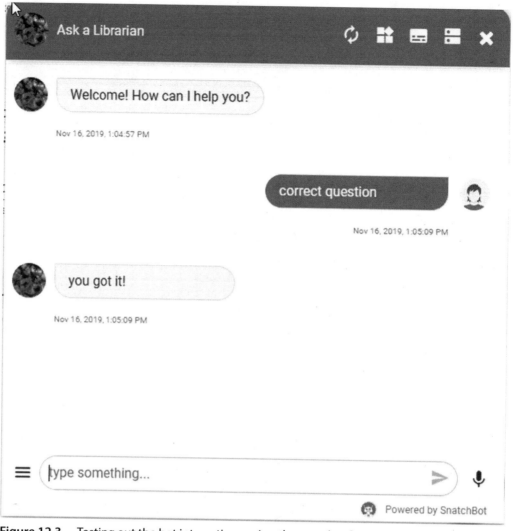

Figure 12.3. Testing out the bot interactions using the test chat feature. *Screenshot of Snatch-Bot interface from snatchbot.me.*

8. To test your bot, click on the image/avatar you uploaded in the lower right corner of the screen. This will expand a test chat where you can interact with your bot.
9. This completes all the steps needed for the trigger of the correct question and the response of the final clue. At this point, you may choose to create more interactions if you want to round out the bot a little and give it more personality or possible responses. Keep in mind that connections should always be set up on the interaction that triggers a certain reply, rather than on the reply, unless the reply has additional triggers to continue the conversation. To view a visual representation of your triggers/connections, click the "Bot scheme" button in the upper right corner of the interface.
10. SnatchBot can operate through a number of different social media or chat platforms, but the easiest option is to get your chat on a webpage you can display or have participants navigate to during the scavenger hunt. To do this, click "Channels" in the far left menu and toggle on the Webchat channel. You can then click over to the "Get embed code" option and either grab the code to embed the chat on a website or use the URL generated for you where SnatchBot will host the bot.

⊚ Lessons Learned

When creating and using chat bots through services like SnatchBot or Botkit, it's important to review the plans and terms. After creating our bot through Botkit, we learned there were only so many messages that could be sent back and forth before the bot would stop working or we would have to pay for some data. The price was fairly inexpensive, so we simply did a one-time payment for the smallest amount of data, and everything worked fine during our event. SnatchBot's pricing page claims the free plan includes unlimited messages, but the Pro plan seems to involve paying for messages, so this would be something to investigate fully before using SnatchBot or another service.

During our scavenger hunt, we set up a public-access computer as a station with the computer already logged in and with a browser open to the correct page. If you go this route, you will need to consider how to prevent participants from seeing the conversations (and correct clues) of previous participants, and how to prevent people from navigating away from the page. An alternate option might be to direct participants to visit the URL on their own devices, but this would exclude anyone without a smart device. Another possibility is assigning a helper to keep watch on this station and to make sure the chat is cleared between participants.

⊚ Variations

This project takes advantage of only a small number of the possible bot features in SnatchBot. There are many ways to make the bot even more involved and interactive, ranging from simply adding more possible responses and interactions to incorporating media or complex logic in the bot's replies. SnatchBot even has plugins that can modify the bot's behavior; for example, there is a Google Calendar plugin that allows users to interact with the bot in order to modify calendar events. Bots can also extract information from users' responses, such as URLs, dates, email addresses, phone numbers, and more. Our version of the Library Services Scavenger Hunt kept it simple, but there are plenty of possibilities to develop and customize a version that works well for you.

Easy-to-edit chat bots can also be extremely useful beyond inclusion in a scavenger hunt like this. The strength of services like SnatchBot and Botkit is the point-and-click visual interface, which allows users to create without needing to understand how to code the bot, or speeds up the process even for those who do know how to program AI. There are even options to incorporate bots into services like Facebook or email, which could allow for an automated and interactive service to respond to patron questions, for example. Bots can also be embedded directly into an existing website (i.e., your library website).

Bonus Projects
Customizable 3-D Printed Pens

THIS PROJECT WAS CREATED at Georgetown University in Washington, D.C. by Beth Campolieto Marhanka (Head of the Gelardin New Media Center & the Maker Hub) and Don Undeen (Manager of the Maker Hub, Georgetown University Library), who provided the information below.

Project Description

To help advertise our new 3-D printers when we first purchased them back in 2015, we were looking for objects made on the 3-D printer that people would like. We also wanted those objects to help advertise the 3-D printing service and ideally be useful as well. 3-D printed pens were the perfect solution for us. A student worker found customizable pen casings on Thingiverse that were a great way to clearly advertise that we had 3D@Lau (we are the Lauinger Library and everyone calls us Lau), and were also useful swag.

◎ Project Audience

The 3-D printed pens were great giveaway items for people we wanted to encourage to use the 3-D printers again, but also for stakeholders around campus we wanted to spread the word to about emerging technologies in the library. They were especially handy for library board members, university administrators, and faculty considering assigning projects in the Maker Hub.

◎ Difficulty Level and Cost

This project is extremely easy. Librarians might find it useful to watch a short tutorial on how to use Tinkercad, but it's not completely necessary. They might also need some instruction on how to use the 3-D printer in their library.

The total cost of each pen is a bit less than 20 cents. The 3-D printed casing only costs a few cents worth of filament. You'll also need to take the ink tube with ballpoint tip out of an inexpensive pen and insert it into the 3-D printed casing you just made. Those pens cost about 15 cents each.

◎ Incorporating the Project

We gave the pens away during meetings with library board members, during tours with donors and university administrators, and also during open house events.

Visitors, board members, and administrators loved getting the pens. We also have other sample 3-D projects to give away, like bracelets and keyrings, but the pens were the most popular.

◎ Credit

- Beth Campolieto Marhanka, Head of the Gelardin New Media Center & the Maker Hub, beth.marhanka@georgetown.edu
- Don Undeen, Manager of the Maker Hub, Georgetown University Library, dhu3@georgetown.edu

◎ Resources

- Access a PDF with full instructions on how to create this project here: http://bit.ly/georgetown3Dpens
- The base model for this project can be found in the Thingiverse collection for this book: https://www.thingiverse.com/sg_librarian/collections/practical-guides-for-librarians-book

Bonus Projects

Tabulatron Stats Tracker

THIS PROJECT WAS CREATED at Onondaga Community College in Syracuse, New York, by Dennis Thoryk (Media Specialist for Coulter Library and adjunct instructor in the computer studies department at Onondaga Community College), who provided the information below.

⊚ Project Description

Our version is an update of the original.[1] The Tabulatron allows staff to keep track of some basic statistical information for our service counters with the press of a button. It uses an Arduino Uno to provide the hardware interface and transmits the signal for each button press through the Arduino's serial connection to a program written in the Processing programming language on the attached computer. The Processing program then sends that data to a Google form and stores it in a Google spreadsheet set up for that service counter.

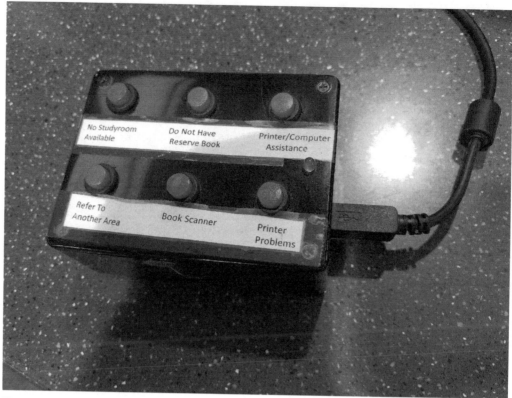

Figure 14.1. One of the Tabulatron tracker devices. *Figure provided by Dennis Thoryk.*

The original consisted of an Arduino Uno in a small project box with two buttons and an LED to provide feedback to the user that the button was pressed. There was also an onscreen GUI (Graphical User Interface) that could be used instead of the Arduino. Our version expanded this to six buttons, updated the GUI to accommodate six choices and modified the Processing code to work with the newer version of Google forms. I built five of these for our three service counters and changed the questions to tailor the data collected to each service counter. Some of the data we collect includes counts on printing assistance, technical questions such as help with the computers, noise complaints, copy machine/scanner assistance, and study room assistance. I summarize the results using pivot tables at the end of each semester.

Project Audience

The project is intended for use by faculty and staff working in the library.

Difficulty Level and Cost

There is programming involved, so the difficulty level is medium to high based on your programming experience.

We spent approximately $200 on the parts to assemble the boxes. This could be reduced some if you 3-D print the project boxes the Arduinos are in instead of purchasing them.

⊚ Incorporating the Project

This project was for staff use. I built one for the reference desk to test and based on their feedback, I adjusted the program and built the rest of them. The project helps us keep track of the service issues that our counters are addressing on a regular basis.

⊚ Credit

- Dennis Thoryk, Media Specialist for Coulter Library and adjunct instructor in the computer studies department at Onondaga Community College.

⊚ Resources

- Tim Ribaric and Jonathan Younker, "Arduino-enabled Patron Interaction Counting," *The Code4Lib Journal 20* (2013), https://journal.code4lib.org/articles/8200.

⊚ Note

1. This was an update of a project found by an Onondaga Community College librarian in the following article: Tim Ribaric and Jonathan Younker, "Arduino-enabled Patron Interaction Counting," *The Code4Lib Journal 20* (2013), https://journal.code4lib.org/articles/8200.

Bonus Projects
State of Sound Kiosk

THIS PROJECT WAS CREATED at North Carolina State University in Raleigh, North Carolina, by Colin Nickels (Experiential Learning Services Librarian), Ty Van de Zande (Graduate Extension Assistant), Justin Haynes (University Library Technician), and Adam Rogers (Head of Making and Innovation), who provided the information below.

 Project Description

Premise

The North Carolina State University Libraries has created a special collection and event series around music and sound created on campus and in the libraries. This collection is still being developed. In order to raise awareness of this collection we wanted to create a physical object that would play selected tracks from the collection. The State of Sound Kiosk was created to highlight and provide another means of access to this collection.

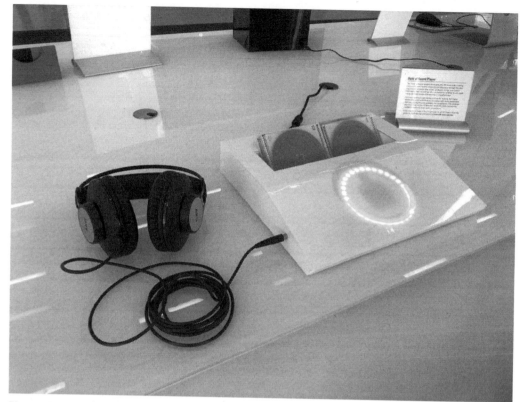

Figure 15.1. The State of Sound Kiosk on display. *Image provided by Colin Nickels.*

Team

We formed a small team to tackle this challenge. Each team member contributed their expertise and experience. Ty Van De Zande, our Graduate Extension Assistant from the College of Design, designed the exterior and interaction; Justin Haynes, Manager of D. H. Hill Jr. Makerspace, laser cut and constructed the enclosure; and Colin Nickels, Experiential Learning Services Librarian, fabricated and programmed the electronics.

Design

This music player's design focuses on skeuomorphically and tangibly displaying a collection of student's music, replicating the vinyl LP experience. The kiosk is an intuitive interaction for choosing music—rather than choosing from a list, the user browses a record crate and plays a song by placing a disc on the player.

Process

Starting with the design, we developed our first prototype to test if we could make a Raspberry Pi respond to RFID using a USB RFID reader. Initially we used NodeRed to test input and outputs. After proving that was possible, we started the search for final hardware, settling on inexpensive RFID readers, tags, and LED rings. We tested different hardware and each new piece added complexity and development time. Ultimately, it was determined that relying on one Arduino and one Raspberry Pi wouldn't support the interactions we designed, so we had to use a second Arduino. Once each hardware piece was defined, we wrote the underlying code so that one Arduino would read the RFID tag and send the information to the Raspberry Pi. The Pi would then check its unique identifier against a list of known tags. If it recognized the tag, it would play the song and send a code to the other Arduino to tell the lights to blink and then spin. If it didn't recognize the tag, then it would send a code to flash red. Getting all these parts to talk to each other predictably was difficult, but creates a unique display that highlights our collection.

What's Next

Right now, the State of Sound Kiosk is a standalone exhibit in Hunt Library, but the renovation of D. H. Hill Jr. Library will open a new space for the State of Sound Kiosk, inside the Innovation Studio. The Innovation Studio will feature interactive projected tabletops. The kiosk will be integrated into a robust technology system that will allow visitors to learn even more about each artist or library resources for music production.

Project Audience

The project is intended for use by students, faculty, staff, and visitors.

Difficulty Level and Cost

As the project requires in-depth knowledge of programming, Arduino, Raspberry Pi, laser cutting, and 3-D printing and design, it is a very difficult project.

Our cost was $35 for the Pi, $10 for a MicroSD Card, $20 for ESP Boards, $10 for an RFID reader, $10 for cables, $25 for 3-D Printer Filament, $5 for RFID Stickers, $80 for Acrylic Enclosure materials, and $10 for LED Ring, totaling $205. You will also need access to a laser cutter and 3-D printer.

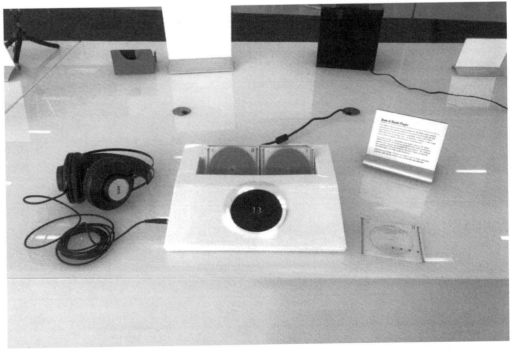

Figure 15.2. The kiosk in action. *Image provided by Colin Nickels.*

◉ Incorporating the Project

This project is currently displayed in our Technology Showcase at James B. Hunt Jr. Library. The State of Sound Kiosk is made using tools in the Libraries' makerspace and features music students from campus have produced. Many of the student tracks were produced using media equipment in the North Carolina State University Libraries, and the project was developed as a connection with the State of Sound event series.

◉ Credit

- Colin Nickels–Experiential Learning Services Librarian at North Carolina State University Libraries–crnickel@ncsu.edu
- Ty Van de Zande–Graduate Extension Assistant–ctvandez@ncsu.edu
- Justin Haynes–University Library Technician–jmhaynes@ncsu.edu
- Adam Rogers–Head of Making and Innovation–asroger2@ncsu.edu

◉ Resources

- North Carolina State University Libraries Technology Showcase Exhibits: https://www.lib.ncsu.edu/spaces/lawrence-ella-apple-technology-showcase/exhibits

How to Be a Great Maker

The Maker Mindset

WHAT MAKES A GREAT MAKER? Just as there is no one-size-fits-all type of makerspace, there is probably no single answer to this question. A lot depends on the individual, and on the type of makerspace a person tends to operate within. There are, however, aspects to thinking like a maker and developing a "maker mindset" that will benefit you in your quest to achieve maker greatness, including (but not limited to) the following ideas and traits:

- Valuing creation over consumption, experiences over artifacts
- Constantly seeking solutions and seeing problems as challenges
- Being willing to experiment and embrace failure as a positive experience
- Being focused on inclusion, access, and equity
- Always seeking out collaborations, partnerships, and opportunities to work with others
- Maintaining an interest in lifelong learning and continual development of new skills

Creation Over Consumption, Experiences Over Artifacts

Since early in the maker movement, there has been a focus on its potential to move away from a culture heavily centered on consumerism toward a culture promoting self-sufficiency and individual creation. A 2009 article describes the "growing community" of maker culture as "a direct reaction to a consumer culture in which most products have become steadily homogenized and local industry has given into big box retailing of dull products made with cheap foreign labor."[1] A piece by Lauren Britton, founder of what is widely considered the first library makerspace (Fayetteville Free Library's Fab Lab), notes, "Maker spaces also acknowledge green concerns by reconnecting consumers to the labor involved in producing what they use."[2]

In keeping with this approach, many popular maker tools are more suited to creating things that are individualized and meant for extended use, rather than disposable and mass-produced. For example, desktop 3-D printers are more ideal for creating a single printed object that a user spends a significant time designing and tweaking for a specific task than for quickly mass-reproducing a cheap object meant to be used up and thrown away. The strength of the maker movement is in moving away from a culture rooted in convenience, cheap labor, and factory production; maker culture is not about making a bunch of generic junk, but is about thoughtful creation of projects meant to last, with a personal touch, and with value and meaning.

Though many associate the maker movement and makerspaces with tools and equipment (3-D printers, CNC machines, sewing machines, robots, and more), another important aspect of maker culture is emphasizing experiences rather than artifacts. It's easy to get excited about flashy new technology and cool projects—and there's a time and place for this—but at its heart, making is about the process of creation and what is gained along the way. Especially in institutions like libraries and schools, makerspaces are not so much about the tangible results but about the new skills, understanding, and confidence that comes with envisioning something and producing it with your own hands.

Seeking Solutions and Seeing Problems as Challenges

Successful makers don't wait around for others to develop solutions or to fix things; they take initiative and seek out creative ways to approach barriers they face. A making mentality is a problem-solving mentality. Whether you are relying on high-tech, complex, or modern equipment for your solutions or utilizing time-tested traditional DIY methods, being a maker means that a problem shouldn't stop you in your tracks, but should encourage you to begin considering, researching, and brainstorming how you might overcome it.

Kurti, Kurti, and Fleming write that "ultimately, the outcome of maker education and educational makerspaces leads to determination, independent and creative problem solving, and an authentic preparation for the real world by simulating real-world challenges."[3] Though their article refers to "educational makerspaces" as a separate concept existing only within educational institutions, all makers benefit from striving toward this goal. Great makers, therefore, know that roadblocks and difficulties are simply challenges waiting for creative solutions, and they get in the habit of responding to these challenges by engaging their strong problem-solving abilities.

Willing to Experiment and Embrace Failure

As a general rule, people don't like to fail, and this is understandable. Failure often carries high stakes and negative consequences. Throughout our lives, we are often punished for failure: bad grades, poor job reviews, interpersonal conflict, and so on. As a result, most people view failure as something entirely bad and to be avoided at all costs.

Failure, however, is very often a key aspect and necessary stepping stone on the road to success. This is a difficult but extremely useful lesson for great makers to learn to embrace. Have you ever gotten lost going somewhere but learned the route better for next time? Gotten crushed fighting an enemy in a video game but picked up details about its patterns and weaknesses for your next attempt? Had a library event turn into a disaster, which led you to change your planning process for next time?

You won't always have the perfect skills or come up with the perfect plan for a project, and that's okay. Making frequently makes use of design thinking, an "innovative problem-solving process" that outlines useful steps to follow when designing solutions or products. One of the most important parts of design thinking is prototyping and iterating a project. MIT Sloan Professor Steve Eppinger describes this stage of the process: "We don't develop a good solution just by thinking about a list of ideas, bullet points and rough sketches . . . We explore potential solutions through modeling and prototyping. We design, we build, we test, and repeat—this design iteration process is absolutely critical to effective design thinking."[4]

Though it's not directly stated, this repeated iteration is actually planned failure. Great makers follow a similar philosophy, understanding that experimentation and multiple attempts are often necessary and even beneficial to successful results. Psychologist Angela Lee Duckworth, in her TED talk about grit, explains, "Dr. Dweck has shown that when kids read and learn about the brain and how it changes and grows in response to challenge they're much more likely to persevere when they fail, because they don't believe that failure is a permanent condition."[5]

Focused on Inclusion, Access, Equity

Making has the potential to teach essential skills and to empower, and these benefits should not be available only to a select few. Being a great maker must include a commitment to inclusion, access, and equity, along with the mindset that making is for everyone. Erin Oldynski, co-founder of feminist makerspace Prototype, explains: "We have people who come to our workshops who have never used a power drill or never written code or never touched a saw before, and they leave our workshops saying, 'this is something I could do, and it's not so intimidating after all.' And that experience, we hope, leads them to pursue further education or training or jobs where they can develop those skills, or to start their own businesses."[6]

Makerspaces can provide equal access to essential STEAM (Science Technology Engineering Art Math) education, to expensive and otherwise unaffordable equipment, and to a community with a wealth of knowledge and connections. Makers can gain confidence and control over their own lives by moving from passive consumption to active creation, gaining the ability to repair and reuse their possessions and to make their ideas a reality.

Great makers are deliberate in their efforts toward inclusion and equity, realizing that intentional work is required to make spaces and community that are inviting for everyone. They recognize that there are many aspects of identity, both visible and invisible, and that people's identities intersect in unique ways. Therefore, great makers care about others' needs, and seek out conversations and relationships with members of marginalized groups to learn more about those needs and how to welcome everyone into the maker movement.

Seeking Out Collaborations and Partnerships

Although the physical act of making something might sometimes be a solitary process (for example, it's fairly challenging to have two people knitting the same scarf at once), the maker mindset is collaborative and focused on working with others. People have been making things throughout human history, and creation in itself is not a novel concept. Much of the recent growth of the maker movement has to do with the deliberately collaborative nature of makerspaces and the way they can bring makers together across barriers such as skill level, age, status, interests, identity, and so on. Makerspaces are often referred to as a "third place," a term coined by sociologist Ray Oldenburg for social environments where people gather other than their homes and workplaces.[7] Cooperation within these spaces has many benefits, including helping people form social connections with each other, leading makers to combine technologies in creative ways, and helping makers develop the skills they need to work successfully in a group.[8] In fact, a lot of popular maker technologies have developed through the type of sharing and collaboration embraced by the maker movement, such as Arduino micro-controllers, a number of 3-D printer models, and a wealth of free and/or open-source software many makers rely on.[9]

A great maker therefore doesn't work in isolation, but actively looks for ways to share ideas, learn about others' work, and form partnerships. To be the most successful, it's also important to consider a maker's commitment to inclusion (outlined above) and seek out the creativity of makers significantly different from yourself in some way. Without reaching across these gaps, makers never would have developed ideas such as wearable electronics, for example, combining the low-tech and traditionally-viewed-as-feminine practice of fabric arts with the high-tech and traditionally-viewed-as-masculine work of circuitry and programming.

Lifelong Learning and Developing New Skills

Above all, to be a truly excellent maker, never stop learning. Tools and technologies change, become obsolete, and are created on a regular basis. There are so many types of making, involving different materials, equipment, and skills. It's impossible to be an expert on everything at once, which is why being a maker is an ongoing, lifelong process of discovery and development. Becoming comfortable should never mean becoming complacent; there will always be more to explore, and great makers embrace this spirit of constant improvement and challenge with an open mind and an excitement for learning.

Important Skills to Develop

This is not intended to be an exhaustive list of all skills makers should develop, nor does it make sense for every maker to have the exact same skills. A lot will depend on the tools available to you, your personal strengths and interests, and the type of projects you plan to create. However, the skills below will serve you especially well in completing projects in this book, and are solid fundamentals that can be useful in a wide variety of situations.

Technical Skills

- Using drills and Dremel, general comfort with power tools
- Soldering
- 3-D printing (3-D design is a plus, but there are many free models available online, which we took advantage of for a number of projects in this book)
- Using a multi-meter to test voltage and current, basic wiring skills such as stripping wire, testing faulty wires
- Arduino programming and using the Arduino IDE (Integrated Development Environment)
- Photo editing and basic graphic design (nicely designed signs and graphics are a great way to enhance many projects)
- Audio and video recording and editing, including knowledge of common formats, file types, codecs, and so on (also useful for documenting projects)
- Sewing (both by hand and with a machine), including knowledge of different stitches and qualities of different fabrics
- Familiarity with different adhesives and their uses

Soft Skills/General Skills

- Adaptability (especially the ability to adapt to changing interfaces of digital tools and software)
- Being good at operating by trial and error, learning from both successes and failures
- Improvisation and the ability to put a personal spin on a project
- Spotting valuable "junk" and repurposing old items
- Knowing how to read and interpret code rather than simply copy/pasting (subskill—helpfully commenting code)
- A spirit of exploration and curiosity

Developing Maker Skills

As with the maker skills list above, this is not meant to be a comprehensive list of all the ways you can develop your skills, but we hope will give you some ideas as to how to begin. There are many resources out there, and new ones are being created all the time.

- Make things! This may seem obvious, but the absolute best way to develop any skill is simply to keep trying and keep practicing. Getting hands-on and making projects for fun, for the purposes of learning, and for any other reason you can think of will go a long way toward helping you expand and hone your expertise.
- Search for resources, especially online. There are lots of books, magazines, and other useful print publications that can lead you through learning technical skills. Sharing and openness are often a core part of maker ideology, however, and the internet makes it very easy for anyone to share videos, tutorials, instructions, guides, digital materials, and more. YouTube can be a good source for tutorials, and sites like Instructables, Make It @ Your Library, Makezine, and Pinterest are excellent for finding projects with step-by-step instructions. Online repositories, such as Thingiverse for 3-D printing, can be helpful in finding digital models or artifacts

to work with. If you're using a specific branded tool, be sure to check if it has an official website with any educational content; for example Arduino's website offers plenty of tutorials and code examples.

- Practice with old, discarded items and things that are cheap or free. Rather than diving in to begin learning something with expensive equipment and materials, get in lots of practice by using items that are no longer needed. For example, try soldering with old electronics that no longer work and drilling with scraps of wood or broken furniture. Ask for donations of fabric scraps or old clothes with holes in them to practice your sewing. Learn graphic design and photo editing basics from free online tools like Canva or Pixlr before investing in expensive software like Photoshop or Illustrator. Once you improve in a particular area, you'll have a better idea of what items you want to spend money on to take your skill to the next level.

- Take things and ideas apart. Tinkering and exploring are excellent ways to develop skills, and there is a lot you can learn by disassembling (and reassembling, if you're able) old equipment. In the same vein, take apart ideas and projects that you come across, as well. If you see something interesting, learn more about how it was created, and practice thinking through how you might achieve something similar. Reverse engineer projects in your head to train yourself to think like a maker and to hone your creativity.

- Start small and focus. Trying to learn or master an array of different skills at once is not only challenging but can be overwhelming. Choose a starting point and set small, achievable goals to help focus your progress. You might prioritize a certain skill or skills, and decide on a simple project to aim for before you focus on learning anything else. Remember that it's okay to develop some of your skills more than others; no one can be an expert in everything, and everyone has various areas in which they're stronger.

- Work with other makers. Find collaborators for projects, and borrow others' expertise while learning from them. Being able to directly tap into other makers' knowledge can be extremely valuable. As everyone has different abilities and strengths, you may even have something to teach them in return.

Tips for Successful Buy-In

While you may be excited to try these projects or other creative maker ideas, it's not always as easy to get other people on board. People may not always see the potential of a project the same way you do, or may have concerns they would like you to address before committing to a project with finances, time, or other resources. Use the suggestions in this section to help put together your own approach for getting buy-in from coworkers and supervisors.

Proof of Concept

It can be difficult to explain an idea and to know if someone is envisioning it the same way you are. Creating proofs of concept can help not only to solidify a nebulous description of a project, but can also help you get a better grasp on possible challenges or anticipate issues you may encounter when beginning the actual project. Proofs of concept can also demonstrate that an idea is feasible and can help you estimate how much work will be involved in the final product.

A proof of concept doesn't need to be a fully working prototype, and the details don't need to fully match the overall vision. Basically, a proof of concept is a scaled down (in size, functionality, or both) version of a project that you can put together relatively quickly to demonstrate how something might take shape. There may be elements that still need to be figured out, perfected, or made to work properly, but your prototype should at least establish that the project is possible, and give a general sense of how it might look when completed. Presenting something like this can do a lot to help others understand your goals and can help build excitement for the eventual completed work.

As an example, while working on the Template Bookmarks project (chapter 3), we created a quick sample bookmark to demonstrate the idea. Our photo backdrop was not yet complete, nor were all the bookmark templates designed, and we hadn't developed the whole workflow of how the bookmarks would be created during the event when we introduced the project. However, we were able to use the sample bookmark as both a goal to work toward and a prototype to show others when explaining what we expected to accomplish. We created a similar proof of concept for our Microsoft Kinect Photo Booth (chapter 6), hacking together a quick setup with the Kinect that projected Juan into a photo of our choosing. There were many details and challenges still to face, but we proved to ourselves and to others that the general idea was viable, and gave ourselves a clear goal for the project's end result.

Collaborating with Others

There are so many good and important reasons to collaborate with others on maker projects, and among them is the possible boost to buy-in it might provide. For one, if more people are involved in a project, there are already more people excited about and committed to the project. Partnerships may also provide an additional source for resources and funding, and can at least double the benefits of a particular project (the end result not only helps you, but your collaborators, as well). If you're working within an academic institution, explore its values and mission statement: administrators often like to see projects that support and involve multiple departments, units, or areas at once. Going outside the confines of your makerspace to find partnerships in the wider community and surrounding maker ecosystem can help you build stronger projects and convince others of the projects' importance.

Every project detailed in this book involved collaboration with others outside our own makerspace, whether those other people were non-makerspace library employees, other units or departments on our college campus, or organizations in our local community. Though we may have done much of the hands-on building, coding, and creating ourselves, we worked with partners for the planning, design, implementation, and integration of the projects. Because we made sure it was clear how our partners would benefit from the collaboration, those partners functioned as advocates, supporters, and helpers along the way.

Levels of Possibility

Another trick for helping with buy-in is to develop plans for a project at two or three levels of possibility and complexity. For instance, what does your ideal version of the project look like? How does that change if you end up with less funding and fewer resources? Thinking through a few potential options and creating flexible plans may help increase the chances that the project gets approved and completed. Rather than being presented with a simple yes or no choice, those you need to convince can better work with you to settle on a version of the project that is feasible for everyone involved.

This approach may also help higher-ups understand why you are asking for a certain budget by breaking down what's possible at different levels of funding. However, don't undervalue what you're doing and ask for less than you need, or you set a standard for future projects you will struggle to reach. The same goes for the amount of time and effort a project will take—make sure to stay realistic about what can be accomplished, and don't be afraid to scale down or simplify projects as necessary to make them happen.

Emphasize Successes

Keeping your project plans reasonable is not only important for initial buy-in and your own mental health but for future buy-in, as well. Your past ability to deliver is likely to be a big consideration in approving future proposals.

After finishing projects, find ways to focus on and emphasize your successes and the benefits of what you've achieved. Create write-ups that can be shared through library newsletters, social media, local or campus news, and so on. If you have collaborators or partners, collect and save anything they share about your project. Record any positive comments or feedback from participants. Find avenues through which you can write about, present on, or otherwise share your successes and the benefits of your work, including conferences and scholarship in the field.

Success does not necessarily have to look like what you expected when you set out to complete the project. Even if things have changed along the way, being an advocate for yourself is important, and will help remind others of what you're capable of, building their trust in you. As you continue to develop project ideas and proposals, a history of proven and documented success will serve you well in getting the support of others.

⦿ Key Points

- To help develop the mindset of a great maker, learn to value creation, experimentation and failure, equity and inclusion, and lifelong learning, while actively seeking out collaborations and developing your problem-solving abilities
- There are lots of fundamental technical skills, as well as soft skills/general skills that are useful to develop as a maker
- Hands-on experimentation, working with others, and seeking out helpful resources are great stepping stones toward developing maker skills
- Tips for successful buy-in can range from creating proofs of concept and "levels of possibility" plans to collaborating with others and emphasizing successes

⦿ References

Britton, Lauren. "The Makings of Maker Spaces, Part 1: Space for Creation, Not Just Consumption." *The Digital Shift*. Oct. 1, 2012. http://www.thedigitalshift.com/2012/10/public-services/the-makings-of-maker-spaces-part-1-space-for-creation-not-just-consumption/.

Kurti, Steven R., Debby L. Kurti, amd Laura Fleming. "The Philosophy of Educational Makerspaces, Part 1 of Making an Educational Makerspace." *Teacher Librarian* 41, no. 5 (2014):

8–11, *Gale General OneFile* (accessed October 25, 2019). https://link-gale-com.ezproxy
.oswego.edu/apps/doc/A373680322/ITOF?u=oswego&sid=ITOF&xid=868caccc.

Linke, Rebecca. "Design Thinking, Explained." *Ideas Made to Matter* (blog). September 14, 2017.
https://mitsloan.mit.edu/ideas-made-to-matter/design-thinking-explained.

McCall, Logan. "What is Maker Culture?" *Yahoo! Voices.* March 10, 2009. http://voices.yahoo.com/
what-maker-culture-diy-roots-2810966.html?cat=46. *Internet Archive.* https://web.archive
.org/web/20130317093545/http://voices.yahoo.com/what-maker-culture-diy-roots-2810966
.html?cat=46.

Ministry of Education. "Inclusion and Collaboration in a Makerspace." *Enabling E-Learning*,
video, 3:09. http://www.elearning.tki.org.nz/Teaching/Future-focused-learning/Makerspaces/
Inclusion-and-collaboration-in-a-makerspace.

Niaros, Vasilis, Vasilis Kostakis, and Wolfgang Drechsler. "Making (in) the Smart City: The
Emergence of Makerspaces." *Telematics and Informatics* 34 (2017): 1145–1148. http://dx.doi
.org/10.1016/j.tele.2017.05.004.

Reed, Amanda. "Feminist Makerspaces: Making Room for Women to Create." *The Riveter.*
February 14, 2018. https://www.therivetermagazine.com/feminist-makerspaces-making
-room-for-women-to-create.

TED. "Grit: The Power of Passion and Perseverance | Angela Lee Duckworth." YouTube Video,
6:12. May 9, 2013. https://youtu.be/H14bBuluwB8.

⑥ Resources

- Instructables – https://www.instructables.com/
- Make It @ Your Library – http://makeitatyourlibrary.org/
- Makezine – https://makezine.com/
- Pinterest – https://www.pinterest.com/
- Official Arduino website – https://www.arduino.cc/
- Adafruit tutorials and projects – https://learn.adafruit.com/ (also check out the blog)
- Thingiverse – https://www.thingiverse.com/
- Yeggi – https://www.yeggi.com/ (search engine for 3-D printable models)

⑥ Notes

1. Logan McCall, "What Is Maker Culture?–DIY Roots," *Yahoo! Voices*, March 10, 2009.
http://voices.yahoo.com/what-maker-culture-diy-roots-2810966.html?cat=46. *Internet Archive.*
https://web.archive.org/web/20130317093545/http://voices.yahoo.com/what-maker-culture-diy
-roots-2810966.html?cat=46.

2. Lauren Britton, "The Makings of Maker Spaces, Part 1: Space for Creation, Not Just Consumption," *The Digital Shift*, Oct. 1, 2012. http://www.thedigitalshift.com/2012/10/public-services/
the-makings-of-maker-spaces-part-1-space-for-creation-not-just-consumption/.

3. Steven R. Kurti, Debby L. Kurti, Laura Fleming, "The Philosophy of Educational Makerspaces, Part 1 of Making an Educational Makerspace," *Teacher Librarian* 41, no. 5 (2014): 8–11,
Gale General OneFile (accessed October 25, 2019). https://link-gale-com.ezproxy.oswego.edu/
apps/doc/A373680322/ITOF?u=oswego&sid=ITOF&xid=868caccc.

4. Rebecca Linke, "Design Thinking, Explained," *Ideas Made to Matter* (blog), September 14,
2017, https://mitsloan.mit.edu/ideas-made-to-matter/design-thinking-explained.

5. TED, "Grit: The Power of Passion and Perseverance | Angela Lee Duckworth," YouTube
Video, 6:12, May 9, 2013, https://youtu.be/H14bBuluwB8.

6. Amanda Reed, "Feminist Makerspaces: Making Room for Women to Create," *The Riveter*, February 14, 2018, https://www.therivetermagazine.com/feminist-makerspaces-making-room-for-women-to-create.

7. Vasilis Niaros, Vasilis Kostakis, Wolfgang Drechsler, "Making (in) the Smart City: The Emergence of Makerspaces," *Telematics and Informatics* 34 (2017): 1145, http://dx.doi.org/10.1016/j.tele.2017.05.004.

8. Ministry of Education, "Inclusion and Collaboration in a Makerspace," Enabling E-Learning, video, 3:09, http://www.elearning.tki.org.nz/Teaching/Future-focused-learning/Makerspaces/Inclusion-and-collaboration-in-a-makerspace.

9. Niaros, Kostakis, and Drechsler, "Making (in) the Smart City," 1148.

Tips and Tricks

◎ Safety

THOUGH THERE CAN BE SOME RISK INHERENT in using equipment like power tools, 3-D printers, soldering tools, and so on, there are simple precautions you can take to keep yourself and others safe in the makerspace. It's also a good idea to develop a set of basic rules and safety procedures that are made publicly available to any users of the makerspace through posted signage, or a document they must sign.

- Read and follow any instructions that come with equipment, including any safety warnings.
- Obtain and wear protective equipment whenever necessary. Safety goggles or glasses are often useful to have, especially when working with power tools. If using sharp tools, considering wearing cut-resistant gloves. Wear clothing that covers and protects you (i.e., closed shoes) and doesn't have long or dangling components that could get caught in a machine.
- Have a first-aid kit on hand and in plain sight.
- Have ready access to a fire extinguisher and know how to use it.
- Clean up after projects to avoid having tools or equipment get in the way or present a danger to others. Make sure to keep floors clear.
- Turn off and unplug devices when they aren't being used. Be careful of where you run cords and cables, and be aware of trip hazards.
- Take care of your equipment. Don't use damaged or broken equipment. Periodically check for frayed or worn out cables.

- When working with electronics and circuitry, be aware of temperature. If components get hot, there is something wrong and you should unplug it or disassemble the circuit immediately. If you see smoke, something is very wrong, and if you do not act, you may cause a fire.
- When drilling wood, pre-drill your holes to avoid splitting the wood.
- Make sure to have the proper amount of ventilation for what you're doing. Be careful of fumes, particulates, and so forth. Wear a breathing mask if necessary.
- Keep all cutting tools sharp and in good condition.
- Repurposing and tinkering with old discarded electronics is an excellent way to learn, but be aware of any potentially hazardous chemicals that could be contained within, such as lead or mercury.
- Secure objects you're working with. Use clamps, stands, vises, and so on, to keep things firmly in place.
- The internet has a wealth of resources from makers who generously share projects, guides, instructions, and digital materials. Make use of this, but approach the information provided with a critical eye. Just because someone has shared something online or created a specific project themselves doesn't mean their advice and methods are safe and accurate.

Obtaining Materials

Sometimes, makerspace equipment can be pricey; however, there are a number of ways to obtain materials for your maker projects that can be simple and cost-effective. Some suggestions are listed below with tips and things to consider when searching for supplies.

Thrift Shops, Second-Hand Stores, Yard Sales

- If possible, negotiate prices to get as much as you can with your budget.
- Find out if items are guaranteed in any way: does the thrift shop have any kind of return policy if electronics don't work, or are items sold as is? Try to test electronics before purchasing them so you know what you're getting.
- Leather can be useful to have around a makerspace, and often can be cheaper to obtain by purchasing old handbags or other leather items you can deconstruct.
- Items like bowls, tupperware, or other small housewares can be useful as storage containers. Suitcases can be used as larger storage containers.
- Think creatively about what you can do with various items. Some things can be stripped down for valuable parts, like motors, LEDs, magnets, sensors, and so on.
- Avoid any battery-powered tool with a rechargeable battery, which often are proprietary, can require special chargers and cables, and might have had its capacity depleted or worn down. An exception would be if you know the rechargeable battery is replaceable, and you know you can get a new one at a good price.
- Thrift shops and yard sales can be a great place to pick up old clothes to use for cosplay, for sewing projects, and as fabric scraps.

Dumpster Diving

- Though it may sound gross, dumpster diving can be an effective way to pick things up cheaply, and to upcycle or reuse items rather than letting them go to waste. People often leave larger items, or items that are in better condition, next to or near a dumpster, rather than inside it, making them easy to retrieve.
- Pay attention to what your own institution throws away. There may be items you can repurpose or take apart for spare parts or raw materials like wood and metal. Though some books weeded by libraries are donated, others can be repurposed for book art projects and so on. Be creative about what you can use and how.
- Be aware of and follow laws about dumpster diving where you live. Check local ordinances and respect "No Trespassing" signs.
- Talk to your IT staff to find out about any technology they are discarding or do not need, and if they're willing to let you have it before it even makes its way to the dumpster.
- If you work on or live near a college campus, a good time to dumpster dive or look for useful discarded items is around when students move out or graduate. Some schools even have more formalized processes by which students can get rid of things they no longer want, so explore these possibilities.

Other options for obtaining materials cheaply include browsing dollar stores, taking donations, and setting up a "junk box" to collect scraps, broken technology, and things people are getting rid of. However, think carefully when deciding to accept donations, as you may want to establish policies for what you will and won't accept. Even with policies, you may spend a lot of time sifting through unusable items or just plain trash.

⌾ Recycling or Reusing Projects

Recycling or reusing projects you've already created is an excellent way to save money on supplies, save time and effort, and be more sustainability-minded. Consider the following suggestions.

- Sometimes, projects are created for a specific event or occasion, then are no longer needed. Other times, makerspace users may abandon projects in the space they no longer want. Take apart these projects for usable materials rather than tossing them or having them take up valuable storage space.
- Make use of materials from failed or unfinished projects and prototypes. Is there something creative you can do with a broken Arduino or 3-D print failures? As an example, we have had students in a ceramics class use failed 3-D prints in their projects to create textures or incorporate into the piece they were working on.
- Tweak, adjust, and reuse projects in their whole form for new purposes. The photo booth project we describe in this book has been through many iterations and has featured in at least eight separate events at our library, serving slightly different purposes each time. We have run it with equipment ranging from an iPod Touch to a Raspberry Pi to a Kinect sensor hooked up to a laptop. Just because a project is "finished" doesn't mean you have to stop working on it and discovering what other potential uses and value it may have.

- Use old projects, completed or not, as learning tools. Studying, taking apart, and building off of projects that are no longer needed can be an educational experience for makerspace users, and can provide a boost to creativity.

Key Points

- Safety can be a concern in a makerspace, but considering possible risks and having established policies and procedures can help a lot.
- There are a number of ways to obtain inexpensive equipment and supplies for your makerspace, including thrift shops, second-hand stores, yard sales, dumpster diving, dollar stores, donations, and junk boxes.
- Maker projects can be reused and recycled in ways that support creativity, education, financial needs, and sustainability.

References

Britton, Lauren. "The Makings of Maker Spaces, Part 1: Space for Creation, Not Just Consumption." *The Digital Shift*. Oct. 1, 2012. http://www.thedigitalshift.com/2012/10/public-services/the-makings-of-maker-spaces-part-1-space-for-creation-not-just-consumption/.

Kurti, Steven R., Debby L. Kurti, and Laura Fleming. "The Philosophy of Educational Makerspaces, Part 1 of Making an Educational Makerspace." *Teacher Librarian* 41, no. 5 (2014): 8–11, *Gale General OneFile* (accessed October 25, 2019). https://link-gale-com.ezproxy.oswego.edu/apps/doc/A373680322/ITOF?u=oswego&sid=ITOF&xid=868caccc.

Linke, Rebecca. "Design Thinking, Explained." *Ideas Made to Matter* (blog). September 14, 2017. https://mitsloan.mit.edu/ideas-made-to-matter/design-thinking-explained.

McCall, Logan. "What Is Maker Culture?" *Yahoo! Voices*. March 10, 2009. http://voices.yahoo.com/what-maker-culture-diy-roots-2810966.html?cat=46. *Internet Archive*. https://web.archive.org/web/20130317093545/http://voices.yahoo.com/what-maker-culture-diy-roots-2810966.html?cat=46.

Ministry of Education. "Inclusion and Collaboration in a Makerspace." *Enabling E-Learning*, video, 3:09. http://www.elearning.tki.org.nz/Teaching/Future-focused-learning/Makerspaces/Inclusion-and-collaboration-in-a-makerspace.

Niaros, Vasilis, Vasilis Kostakis, and Wolfgang Drechsler. "Making (in) the Smart City: The Emergence of Makerspaces." *Telematics and Informatics* 34 (2017): 1145–1148. http://dx.doi.org/10.1016/j.tele.2017.05.004.

Reed, Amanda. "Feminist Makerspaces: Making Room for Women to Create." *The Riveter*. February 14, 2018. https://www.therivetermagazine.com/feminist-makerspaces-making-room-for-women-to-create.

TED. "Grit: The Power of Passion and Perseverance | Angela Lee Duckworth." YouTube Video, 6:12. May 9, 2013. https://youtu.be/H14bBuluwB8.

Index

About the Authors

Juan Denzer is a Discovery Services Librarian at SUNY Oswego. He is a graduate of Binghamton University with a bachelor's degree in computer science and a master's degree in library and information science at Buffalo University. He is the author of *Digital Collections and Exhibits* and has contributed to *Escape Rooms and Other Immersive Experiences in the Library* and *63 Ready-to-Use Maker Projects*.

He enjoys making projects for the library and helping students with their ideas. He actively seeks out other academic and public libraries for inspiration. He has presented at Computers in Libraries, Charleston Library Conference, and Internet Librarian. He was also invited to speak at the ELI EDUCAUSE Annual Meeting for his work with the Leap Motion device and Rare Books collection called the Athenaeum in Motion Project (https://bit.ly/2p5JMfu.).

Sharona Ginsberg is head of the Learning Commons at the University of Maryland, College Park. Previously, she was the Learning Technologies Librarian at SUNY Oswego, where she founded and facilitated the library makerspace. She is a graduate of Ithaca College with a bachelor's degree in English and the University of Michigan School of Information with a master's degree in information (specializing in library and information science). She has been doing work in the field of library makerspaces since 2012. She was a 2015 recipient of the *Library Journal* Movers & Shakers award for her work on Maker-Bridge, a website and blog devoted to the maker movement in libraries and schools.

She has shared her work at numerous conferences on the international, national, regional, and local levels, including ALA Annual and ISAM (the International Symposium on Academic Makerspaces), and has been invited to speak on the topic of makerspaces in libraries. Her recent publications include contributions to *The Makerspace Librarian's Sourcebook* and *Creative Instructional Design: Practical Applications for Librarians*. She also reviews comics and graphic novels for the website *No Flying No Tights* (http://www.noflyingnotights.com) and enjoys spending time with her partner, Charlette, and her dog, Bilbo Waggins.